"Jeremy helps us to eagerly desire pr[...] through his new book. He not only [...] through fresh teaching, he also helps [...] will be especially helpful to leaders [...] who has paid a price for his own prop[...] this easy-to-read, insightful book."

Shawn Bolz, senior pastor, Expression58;
author, *Keys to Heaven's Economy* and
The Throne Room Company; www.expression58.org

"Jeremy Lopez has a true desire to help people connect with God through the Holy Spirit. His unique ability to communicate with simplicity is needed in the Church today. I highly recommend his ministry and training resources."

Doug Addison, InLight Connection;
www.dougaddison.com

"Jeremy Lopez has a unique writing style of simplicity that communicates the truth of God in a clear and concise way. He demystifies what it means to be a prophet and the characteristics that accompany a prophet, and he makes them understandable to the reader. Jeremy is very balanced and scripturally sound in his approach to the prophetic ministry, and he clearly outlines why we must have it in operation in our midst today. As Jeremy shows, being a prophet is not easy, but well-respected prophets are a much-needed asset to the Body of Christ."

Randy Clark, Global Awakening;
www.globalawakening.com

"In this book, *Releasing the Power of the Prophetic*, Jeremy Lopez brings to the readers his revelatory insight into the prophet's ministry. It is written with honesty and simplicity to help everyone to receive from this most needed ministry today. As the desire to know more about prophets and their flow in the Spirit grows, this book will be one of the great helps."

Roberts Liardon, Roberts Liardon Ministries;
www.robertsliardon.org

"God is awakening a generation to the realms of the Spirit. He is giving eyes and ears to a company of people who will hear His voice and respond to His heart. In this book, Jeremy Lopez gives valuable insights for activating your spiritual senses and engaging heaven. The prophets, seers and forerunners of old have laid foundational blueprints for the 21st-century Church to build upon. As you read this book, position yourself to encounter the same Spirit of Revelation that the fathers of our faith knew, bringing forth the power and demonstration of God's Kingdom in your own life!"

John Crowder, Sons of Thunder Ministries and Publications;
author, *Miracle Workers, Reformers* and *The New Mystics*;
www.thenewmystics.com

"This work is a much-needed foundational yet insightful look at the prophetic and revelatory ministry. Jeremy Lopez does a great job not simply rehashing what's already out there, but bringing some fresh nuggets that will surely yield an impartation of the prophetic. This work is much like the hand of Elisha on his servant (see 2 Kings 6:17) that yielded open eyes to perceive in the spirit realm and was a catalyst of fresh faith. I trust that this easy-to-read yet profound book will catapult you to new levels of revelatory release. Let's take this spiritual weaponry to the streets and see a marketplace revolution released."

Sean Smith, Sean Smith Ministries;
www.seansmithministries.org

"We're living in a time when there needs to be clear revelation coming from a seasoned prophetic generation that will bring genuine answers to the world we live in with striking accuracy. This book by Jeremy Lopez brings definition and helpful insights into the understanding of the Spirit of Prophecy. I fully recommend it."

Jeff Jansen, Global Fire Ministries International;
www.globalfireministries.com

"God is raising up true sons that are after His heart and know His voice, being filled with the pure expression of His love. You will find a treasure of insights and principles on living the prophetic life and functioning in the prophetic through this new book!"

John Belt, Live in His Presence Ministries;
www.liveinhispresence.com

"In Jeremy's volume, *Releasing the Power of the Prophetic,* we see an unusual combination of the teacher mantle and prophetic mantle operating harmoniously to bring the necessary revelation to the movement. Thank God for people like Jeremy who pay the price for the authentic. You will gain insight and understanding reading *Releasing the Power of the Prophetic,* as I did."

David Tomberlin, David Tomberlin Ministries;
www.davidtomberlin.com

"If you desire to know the balanced understanding of walking in the prophetic anointing of God, you could not have a better source than *Releasing the Power of the Prophetic*. Jeremy Lopez is a proven prophetic voice for God that offers knowledge in this wonderful prophetic guidebook.

"*Releasing the Power of the Prophetic* is brought to you by someone with years of Bible-based prophetic preaching and teaching who has utilized the gifts and office of the Lord with integrity."

John Mark Pool, Word to the World Ministries;
www.w2wmin.org

"With wisdom and clarity, Jeremy Lopez presents the prophetic principles that have been the foundation of his own achievements. He explains how the prophetic can be a cornerstone to a successful prophetic-filled life, success based on God's guidelines. Written with simplicity and depth that will have life-changing effects, this book will catapult your spirit into a higher dimension of key understanding."

Brian Lake, Brian Lake Ministries;
www.brianlake.org

"The prophetic is a powerful *tool,* when used properly, to bring comfort and encouragement to those who are crying out for answers. In the hour in which we are living, it is imperative for us to know the voice of God and be quick to obey when He speaks. Jeremy Lopez brings incredible insight to this often-misunderstood gift. He speaks out of his years of moving in the prophetic and gives keys that demystify prophetic ministry, making it practical and attainable. I wholeheartedly recommend this book to you. God does nothing without first speaking to His servants the prophets."

André Ashby, Soul's Cry Ministries;
www.soulscry.org

"I have received many prophetic words from Prophet Jeremy Lopez. The first one was great and the second one had me crying with joy. I will continue to sow seeds into your ministry because it is awesome. The prophetic word was so accurate."

Jimmy Spencer, #33,
former player for the Denver Broncos

RELEASING THE POWER

of the
Prophetic

*A Practical Guide to Developing
a Listening Ear and a Discerning Spirit*

JEREMY LOPEZ

Chosen
a division of Baker Publishing Group
Minneapolis, Minnesota

Copyright © 2011 by Jeremy Lopez

Published by Chosen Books
11400 Hampshire Avenue South
Bloomington, MN 55438
www.chosenbooks.com

Chosen Books is a division of
Baker Publishing Group, Grand Rapids, Michigan.

Printed in the United States of America

Library of Congress Cataloging-in-Publication Data

Lopez, Jeremy, 1970–
    Releasing the power of the prophetic : a practical guide to developing a listening ear and a discerning spirit / Jeremy Lopez ; foreword by James W. Goll.
        p.   cm.
    ISBN 978-8007-9521-4 (pbk. : alk. paper)
    1. Prophecy—Christianity. I. Title.
BR115.P8L67 2011
234'.13—dc22   2011025240

11   12   13   14   15   16   17   7   6   5   4   3   2   1

I dedicate this book to my Lord and Savior Jesus Christ, my rock and my shield, the glory and the lifter of my head. Without You I would be nothing, but with You I can accomplish anything. Thank You for Your grace, mercy and love upon my life. May Your Kingdom come and Your will be done on earth as it is in heaven. As Isaiah once said, "Here I am, send me." Use me to display Your glory in the earth until every nation is filled with You and only You.

This book is also dedicated to my parents, Pastors Jim and Jeannie Lopez. You both are the best example of God's love I have ever known. You have been my inspiration and anchor through the good and the bad. May the glory of God continue to shine upon you both with grace, mercy and peace all the days of your lives. I love you very much.

Contents

Foreword

The book you hold in your hand is a miniature encyclopedia of the operation of the Spirit of Prophecy from *A* to *Z*. Jeremy Lopez's life, ministry and writings are the fruit of a generation that has grown up in a supernatural culture. If it is true that my generation's ceiling becomes the next generation's floor, then Jeremy is standing right on top of my head!

Jeremy ministers from having lived a life dedicated to the Lord Jesus Christ. His gifting is an overflow of a life of intimacy spent before the feet of his beloved. He has drunk from many streams, honors the fathers and mothers in the Spirit who have gone before him and yet realizes he must—and does—stand in the security of his own calling and his own gifting.

Early on a solid pastor told him, "Jeremy, always remember God desires to talk to His people." Wow! I wish someone had assured me like that when I was a teenager. Instead, I had to stumble along and basically learn on my own. I learned by trial and error. There were *no* major books on the prophetic to read when I was coming up. There were *no* prophetic conferences or classes, let alone a school of the supernatural! But times have changed! And the generations are being joined in content, experience and revelation. Awesome!

The wisdom contained in this transparent read alone could help many budding prophets from detonating and destroying themselves and the church congregations and individuals that they attempt to minister to. Writing from years of experience, Jeremy tackles topics like a player in a football game. Everything from "What is this 'prophets' and 'prophecy' stuff?" to "What does a prophet do?" is covered. In another scrimmage you get playing-field time on the subjects of "Oh no! I think I received a wrong word!" and "I received a prophetic word—now what?" I love the candid nature of this generation and the tone contained in this book. It is both real and challenging!

I am one who has dedicated his life and ministry to helping equip prophets and intercessors in a global manner. I am constantly developing tools to transfer the prophetic and intercessory spirit to the many—not just to an elite few. I continue to keep my eyes open for next-generation emerging leaders that I can buddy up to and in a relational manner share a few insights. Many of them walk in levels of gifting I never have. Many of them receive detailed words of knowledge I rarely do. But I stand secure in my role.

My primary role today is to be a coach and a cheerleader to those coming forth. And from that position by the playing field, I declare, "Run with the ball, Jeremy! Run! You got it, buddy. Now score on behalf of the whole team!"

Perhaps that is what this book will do in your life. Is that not what the true prophetic spirit is all about? I read in here that the prophetic gifting ultimately is to edify, exhort and bring comfort. If that is the goal, then this book just scored!

God bless each of you!

James W. Goll,
founder, Encounters Network and Prayer Storm
International; author, *The Seer, The Lost Art of Intercession,
The Coming Israel Awakening* and many others

Preface

*T*he topic of prophecy is surrounded and weighed down by misconceptions and personal experiences that range from miraculous to devastating. Mystics, occasionally, talked about "the cloud of unknowing," and this is truly what prophecy is for most of us. Murky. Mysterious. Misunderstood. My hope is to cast light through those clouds, whether they be inexperienced opinions that fog our judgment or misguided personal familiarity. If we want to truly understand this amazingly vast and beautiful topic, it is important to filter those experiences and teachings as you read this book and seek to discover what is true or false within your own conceptions.

The power of the prophetic is rooted in Scripture, yet it has been squelched or outright denied for generations. Prophecy, as related to signs and wonders and gifts of the Spirit, has widely been denounced as heresy for much of Christian history. The Church fathers have, historically and presently, debated whether gifts of the Spirit such as tongues or prophecy are still active in or relevant to the present time. There are entire denominations built around the "fact" that God's Spirit is no longer dynamically on the move or at work the way He was in Scripture. Votes have often been taken that signs and wonders were "closed" at the completion of the biblical canon and with the death of the apostles (as if a human democratic vote has the final word on whether God's active and present purpose is real and alive).

This book is not meant to join the assortment of arguments for or against prophecy. In truth it is meant to encourage followers of Christ to consider, either for the first time or once again, the power of God and the profound relevancy of His Spirit. A wise man once said, "Trust in the LORD with all your heart and lean not on your own understanding; in all your ways submit to him, and he will make your paths straight" (Proverbs 3:5–6). Trusting in Him and submitting our minds to His Spirit is the theme of this book. Straight paths are not clearly marked on our own maps. Human maps, as human ingenuities, lack lasting legitimacy or deep connection to the underlying reality of what is at work. In light of this, it is the power of the prophetic that is our link to God's maps—God's ways that are not our ways, God's thoughts that are, always, far above.

The life of a believer should be evidenced by process, by development, by growth along a certain set of lines. "Get wisdom, get understanding," Scripture tell us (Proverbs 4:5). "Though it cost all you have, get understanding. Cherish her, and she will exalt you; embrace her, and she will honor you. She will give you a garland to grace your head and present you with a glorious crown" (Proverbs 4:7–9). We are not born with all the wisdom in the world gathered in our beings. Just as a child must develop cognitively from being incapable of so much to competency in navigating the world, so too the spiritual man moves from infancy to maturity. When we submit to Christ and the plans of God, the whole storehouse of wisdom and knowledge are thrown open to us. We are invited to seek that which is more precious than gold or rubies. The heart of God and the mind of the Spirit are offered to us freely through the work of Christ. While it is without doubt a process, there is much we have been given in the Now of God (which I have written about elsewhere). With this in mind, I am writing this book in agreement with Proverbs. If you are seeking to follow Jesus, then you are invited to discover the truth in all things. You are invited to find wisdom.

The disciple Matthew, who spent years living with and listening to Jesus, tells us:

> "Ask and it will be given to you; seek and you will find; knock and the door will be opened to you. For everyone who asks receives; the one who seeks finds; and to the one who knocks, the door will be opened.
>
> "Which of you, if your son asks for bread, will give him a stone? Or if he asks for a fish, will give him a snake? If you, then, though you are evil, know how to give good gifts to your children, how much more will your Father in heaven give good gifts to those who ask him!"

Matthew 7:7–11

My hope is that you, the reader, would ask Him for knowledge of the truth and His own wisdom—in fact, ask for God Himself *as* Wisdom, as you read this book. In every page, I pray you discover that which is true and good and pure, and if there are things that trouble or confuse you, that you would submit those ideas to God Himself and ask for His clarification. He is good to those who wait on Him; it is good to wait patiently for the Lord. As you wait, may you rise up on eagles' wings to breathe the fresh air of heaven.

Acknowledgments

My prayer is that everyone begins to awaken to hear the voice of a loving God who does not condemn but loves unconditionally. When you are in relationship with Him, you will begin to discover He loves you and wants the very best for you. I wrote this book for all who desire to hear His voice and follow.

I want to thank Pastor John Smallwood for your friendship and support through the years. Your guidance and wisdom have been a godsend. You truly have been a friend who sticks closer than a brother.

I would also like to thank the staff of Identity Network for making this project possible. It would not have been except for your hard work and dedication, pushing me and encouraging me to follow my heart and write to those who desire to learn of a loving Father to all His people. May His grace shine upon you guys always.

Finally, I want to give thanks to God for my family, for your love and support and for giving me life to express the Father's love while on this earth.

1

"You Want Me to Say What???"

A prophetic word can shake mountains and yet change lives at the same time.

We live in a day and age when things are accelerating all around us. It is as though time herself is racing toward the arms of her Maker. Change is happening exponentially; even the exponents are changing. I witness this happening in the natural realm; do you think the heavenly realm is accelerating, too? If it is, how would we know? How can one develop eyes to see what eyes cannot possibly see?

If you are like me, you might be wondering, *Does God sit in heaven and wait until we die to arrive, or does He want to talk and communicate with us now, bringing heaven to earth?* The answer is yes, of course, God is there to meet us when this veil of physical matter is removed. But He desires to and delights in talking to each and every one of us—right here, right now. Is that not incredible? It speaks of both God's greatness and God's goodness. Abba's

19

heart for us is unlimited. His voice is unstoppable. And in Christ, His love manifests itself in His incarnation, birth, life, teachings, miracles, death, resurrection, ascension and indwelling. Through this divine chain of events, held together by the Holy Spirit in His very being, Jesus is drawing us even now into His home (heaven) to have a relationship with us forever—and that relationship begins right now.

The triune God is eager to raise up vessels (ordinary people) who share the deepest secrets of His heart. God is raising up a company of holy couriers carrying the very oracles of God (see 1 Peter 4:11, NKJV). At the end of the day, operating in the prophetic is becoming God's friend. When we cultivate a supple heart, eyes to see and ears to hear, we will hear our beloved Friend speaking renewed life, intimacy and power into our lives so that we become living letters, written in large and unmistakable script, telling a simple story penned by the author and finisher of our faith. God loves us, has a plan for our lives and is calling us to become the full embodiment of God's answer to our prayer: "May Your Kingdom come, Your will be done on earth as it is in heaven." This is indeed a time of great change. Our call is nothing less than to glorify God and participate in the healing of creation. Can you imagine anything more exciting than that?

My Life in the Prophetic

As a young teenager I was a member of a small charismatic church. The gifts of the Spirit were well known to us, and I had seen many evidences of His Spirit. I know that many people have difficult experiences in church. Mine, too, were all too human; but many loved the Lord more than anything. I will never forget how one day God spoke to me and told me that He wanted to use me to speak to others. I felt a particular inner prompting that day that was unlike anything else I had felt before.

This call is received in different ways by different people; I, for one, had no problem with it at all. I was just excited that the Lord spoke to me! I would have done anything that voice told me to do. Knowing that the Creator God of the universe takes personal interest in you, caring and communicating His purpose and person, is a phenomenal experience! I felt His prompting to share a message with the congregation publicly. During our time of praise and worship, I slowly went up the aisle. I looked at my pastor and told him, "The Lord told me to say something to someone here." The pastor knew God had His hand upon my life, so he said, "The platform is yours." *Now* I was scared! I made my way up to the platform in front of the worship team and the watching congregation.

Prompted by unusual boldness, I pointed to an older gentleman and said, "I see two doors. One door has your wife in it, and the other door has another woman in it. I see you going from door to door. What does that mean to you?"

You could have heard a pin drop. I wondered if I did the right thing. In truth I had no idea at all what the Lord was saying through me, especially as a young teenager speaking to an older man, but he understood what was being said. He immediately stood up and told me I was wrong and that I had missed God completely. Then he stormed out.

Can you imagine? I was horrified and had no idea what to do. I knew I was called to be a prophet, but I had little clue as to what this meant and even less of a clue as to how people around me would respond. I went home that night upset and discouraged, telling my parents, "I will never speak for God again." It was not as though I doubted God's speaking; rather the outcome was so discouraging I could not imagine repeating the experience another time. Fortunately (as it turned out), my high school was affiliated with my church, so everyone at school knew about the drama of that week's service. The next day in school, the principal called me out of the classroom and told me to come to the office with him. This could not be a good sign. I thought, *Oh no, what have I done?*

When we reached the principal's office, he told me I had a phone call. It was my pastor.

He said, "Remember that man you prophesied to last night?" I swallowed hard, my mind racing with fear. In spite of my distress, I

21

said yes. He said, "That man called me this morning crying, telling me he was sorry, but he was living in adultery, and that the young man last night was correct."

I did not know whether to cry or shout.

I will never forget the words my pastor imparted to me that day: "Jeremy, always remember that God desires to talk to His people. Sometimes He will say things that will not feel good, and sometimes He will tell us things that make us feel great; but either way, it will *always* be for our good in the long run. And when spoken out of a pure and sincere heart of love, it will always call people to repentance."

This was one of my first experiences as a prophet. I anguished over the intensity of the word I delivered—and I am quick to admit that a personal message shared in public is not the usual way the Lord directs His children. But God had a loving plan for that man that was far better than the hurtful and duplicitous relationship he was apparently involved in. While I am thankful that God used me in such a way, I will also add that God rarely seems to move in such a publicly exposing manner. The prophetic is most often dynamically encouraging—explicitly constructive.

Later reflecting on this early, powerful prophetic utterance, I asked God, "Why did You use a young guy to say something so profound to an older gentleman?" And the Lord seemed to say, quite simply, *Not everyone wants to or is tuned in to listening to Me when I speak. But as long as you have a pure, gentle, genuine heart that is so ready to hear, I will speak every time. I want My people to know My love toward them. Will you allow Me to use you to do that all the days of your life?*

I was amazed. My answer was then, and is still, absolutely, "Yes, Lord. Here am I. Send me."

2

We Must Shift This Hour

The prophetic word comes in seed form, packed full of the next chapter of your life.

In the midst of exponential change—technological, ecological, demographic (with more global youth alive now than at any other point in human history), social (as women and those in the Two-Thirds World are more educated and are taking charge over their destiny more than ever before)—God is opening our eyes to the place in the Spirit where He desires to take the Church in this hour. God's manifest destiny—His ultimate intention—and highest calling are breaking forth into the highways and byways, bubbling up through the cracks and the least expected places. The Spirit is stirring in the earth; can we hear Him in our sanctuaries—in our houses of the holy? God is pouring out waves of unconditionally overwhelming, lavish passion on His sons and daughters and unstinting grace into the streets. Can you feel it where you are sitting right now? You may be thinking that this is "hype" or "upselling."

Truth be told, I cannot oversell this point. I can hardly begin to tap in to the inexhaustible and glorious riches of what God is doing in the here and now. God is on the move. Hallelujah!

There is a call to "come up higher" in the things of the Lord. In these days that, I believe, rival the glories of Pentecost, God is pouring out His Spirit on all flesh. The living and cosmic Christ is moving us from one realm of glory into another. "And we all, who with *unveiled faces* contemplate the Lord's glory, are being transformed into his image with ever-increasing glory, which comes from the Lord, who is the Spirit" (2 Corinthians 3:18, emphasis added). This verse is so common it can easily be skipped over. Don't. There is a collective statement at work here: "We *all* . . . with unveiled faces . . ." We *all*—that is the Church! That is our grandparents and spouses and sons and daughters and friends and neighbors . . . that is all of us! Not only that, but many translations use the singular "face." We are being seen as a great whole: one work, one sweeping mission. God does not have many purposes. God does not have many little things He is about. Hardly. God is moving in a special and unique way, and it takes the form of one distinct and powerful purpose. What is it? Continue on in this verse: As we "contemplate the Lord's glory," we "are *being* transformed into . . . ever-increasing glory"! God is doing a makeover! God is remodeling the house. God is taking that which is old and tired and bursting apart and making it new—just as He makes all things new. This is His purpose, and the means by which that purpose is accomplished are quite simple; they could not be more obvious, in fact. The unique mechanism for God's redemptive and transformative work is wrapped up in beholding Him, or as the verse says, "contemplat[ing] the Lord's glory."

Do we see it, or are we playing our same tired religious games? This is not a word of condemnation but a divine dare: Do *you* dare burst out of your in-group ghetto to see how the Creator is birthing new creation in the midst of a tired and broken world? Do I? How hungry are we, you and I? Are we hungry and thirsty enough to open ourselves to beholding our Lord—to contemplating His presence?

In order to see what is really happening, we need divine eye salve (see Revelation 3:18); we must allow the Spirit to change our perception of things in this hour. New sight requires new eyes. The prophetic office, gift and movement are pouring out like fire across the earth today. When the voice of the Lord speaks, it brings change, elevation, new perception and enlightenment to everything it touches. Allow yourself to be not merely an instrument; drink deeply of your destiny as a son or daughter of God being raised up for such a time as this. He is raising up His sons and daughters as never before. He is raising up trumpets to sound the alarm with the same fire that was in Jeremiah. His word will be like fire shut up in your bones. The prophetic, unleashed as we come before the Lord—beholding Him, contemplating Him—is the key to witnessing what God is doing today and to being a part of it.

What is happening in our midst reminds me of an ancient Christian parable from the Desert Mothers and Fathers (women and men who were accustomed to spending time before the throne of the Most High): Abba Lot went to see Abba Joseph and said to him, "Abba, as far as I can, I keep my daily prayers. I fast a little. I pray. I meditate. I live in peace and, as far as I can, I purify my thoughts. What else can I do?"

The old man stood up and stretched his hands toward heaven. His fingers became like ten lamps of fire, and he said to him, "Why not be changed into fire?"

Why not, indeed? That is exactly what God is inviting us to do today. To be consumed with His fire, with His truth, with His vision—setting the world ablaze.

Adam, Walk with God Again

Throughout Scripture, the Spirit of God interacts and speaks with people in different ways. First He communed with Adam as naturally as we spend time with friends. After sin entered the world, the Spirit of God could no longer dwell on earth in the same way. Because God cannot abide sin, He no longer could interact with man on such a casual level. Yet He never stopped loving His creation and wanting to restore relationship with it. In the Old Testament, we see the Spirit of God falling and resting "on" people. These are examples of the Spirit of God visiting people in what may not be quantifiable ways but are time-oriented ways. After Pentecost, though, we see a change in the events of Scripture. The Spirit of God indwells His people again. He comes directly Himself in tongues of fire and in the laying on of hands (see Acts 2:1–4; 8:17). God has found a way to restore direct communication with His people.

Since Adam was the first person to hear the voice of the Lord, I consider him the first prophet. In Genesis it says Adam walked with God "in the cool of the day" (Genesis 3:8). *The Message* says that God was strolling in the "evening breeze." The word *cool* in the Hebrew contains the same root as the word *Spirit*. Adam walked with God in the Spirit. I love that imagery because an actual physical feeling is attached to it. I become aware of a particular sensation when I think of the cool of the day. I feel the breeze drift over my skin. I hear the wind casually enliven the leaves, moving them, stirring them. Inwardly I am suddenly at rest. I feel calm. I am centered. This is the biological experience of being in the Spirit. This is what God wants to restore—or, as I like to describe it, to *awaken:* the relationship and intimacy Adam had with God. Divine-human fellowship was broken in Eden, but it was restored in Christ, the second Adam, the perfect man in whose nature we partake. We are now elevated to the same level of fellowship promised to Adam and Eve in Eden: in the New Covenant, we sit in heavenly places *in* Christ (see Ephesians 2:6; Romans 5:1–2; 2 Peter 1:3–4). We walk with God, in Spirit, allowing the peace that surpasses all intuition or common sense to be at home within our day-to-day experience.

There is a place in God that calls to us. Allow the Holy Spirit to awaken you to the place that Adam understood—the place of sonship, or of being God's child. Do not wait. Do it this hour. "Today, if you hear his voice, do not harden your hearts" (Hebrews 3:7–8). Sons know the voice of their Father; sheep know the voice of their Shepherd. God is our Abba, our friend and the lover of our souls. The prophetic has everything to do with these identities of God, and it draws us into all these dimensions of divine relationship. We are brought into the realm of hearing our Daddy cry, "Come on, climb into My lap [see Hebrews 4:16]. Come, walk with Me." We are called to kinship with Jesus as our Lord, but we are also called with Him as our brother. "Come and find out what I have in store for you," says the Lord. "Come and know the joy, the journey and the abundance of life that I died to give you while on this earth." The Spirit and the Bride together say, "Come." That is really the point. Deep calls to deep as we are invited into the never-ending dance of Father, Son and Holy Spirit.

The same Spirit of God who strolled with Adam in the cool of the day is the same Spirit who raised Christ from the dead, and He is the same Spirit who dwells in you. He desires to breathe new life into the dried-out husks of your life, raising you from the dead to hang out with Daddy in worship and adoration. When you walk "in" and not "with" the Holy Spirit, you shift from Old Covenant law (when the Spirit would be "on" someone) to New Covenant abundance (in which God's law is written on our hearts, and the Spirit unites us in divine oneness [see 1 Corinthians 6:17]). You begin to see God from a different angle. It is as Paul recognized in Athens: In Him you live, move and have your being (see Acts 17:28). The source has changed from exterior to interior—from separate, remote and removed into fully engaged, invested and vital.

Do you desire to start living life to the fullest and have the victory everywhere you go? Do you desire to begin walking the life of faith without growing weary—drinking water that will not ever run dry? Then let's delve deep into your identity so you can begin to live in the Spirit, as the first Adam was created to and the last Adam did perfectly.

Begin to walk in the depths of God. These depths have a name: the Holy Spirit. The prophetic release will begin to take you past the shame-filled avoidance that caused Adam to try to hide from God into the grace-saturated, holy presence of God, where His heart speaks to you "face to face," with face unveiled. This is where Christ opens you up like a living epistle, or love letter, and pours His creativity, thoughts and mind into the book of your life. The Word says that we are living epistles read by everyone (see 2 Corinthians 3:2). Living with a prophetic anointing unleashes the Holy Spirit to write words, sentences and chapters in the book of your life. You will be filled to overflowing with Daddy's goodness, love and compassion. He is not just calling you to be "read by everyone" but to speak His words and dreams into the lives of others so their "books" will also burn with His purpose, presence and destiny.

Knowledge of the Prophetic

Knowledge of the prophetic office and common gifting are key to operating in excellence when you are speaking for God. Without the keys to the prophetic—that is, education, proficiency, practice and wisdom in prophetic operation—we can bruise, hurt and ultimately destroy a life crying out for help. Remember my first experience with the prophetic that I described earlier? While God certainly used it, I have learned since then that a degree of sensitivity and grace, even God-sanctioned privacy, does great help in making strides once the restorative work begins. Otherwise the rubble is far greater and far more scattered than need be. How we act on God's command can be just as important as the "what" of the command itself. This requires understanding, a true knowledge of God's will and His way. God wishes to have people who are empowered to both ends. Scripture says that there is a famine in the land for the speaking of God; we are destroyed for lack of knowledge (see Amos 8:11; Hosea 4:6). It is not that God is reticent to speak; it is that we have been slow to understand. But God our Healer stands at the gate of our understanding; actionable knowledge will end our suffering.

Knowledge is the key to the prophetic that will help open up the spiritual doors for you to walk in excellence and integrity and to show the majesty of God in all you do.

Scripture speaks of keys. Keys have the power to open and to keep shut. They have the power to bind and to loose heavenly realities—as above, so below. Knowledge sought in humility helps you understand the thing you are seeking. It is as Jesus instructs us:

Ask and it will be given to you; seek and you will find; knock and the door will be opened to you. For everyone who asks receives; those who seek find; and to those who knock, the door will be opened.

Matthew 7:7–8, TNIV

When you begin to turn the key of knowledge, you will find "openings" you never thought existed. Knowledge is the key to opening the things you desire—the things that God Himself desires. The prophetic in this hour needs the key to open up the heart of God so we can feel the beat and rhythm of His glory. The prophetic will release His thoughts, His passion and His resurrection power toward us and all creation. Prophetic people in this hour are attuned to a shift like the world has never known before. As we are built together in real prophetic community, our mantle will be strong as it drips with God's likeness. Our fragrance will smell like the rose of Sharon. And the words that come out of our mouths will speak of hope stemming from the promises that are "yes and amen" for humanity that is awakening to God's lavish grace. All this is the outcome of true and discerning knowledge.

Speaking As a New Covenant Prophet

Prophets must realize this hour that our source is a covenant of grace and not law. Do yourself a favor and spend some time today, maybe even this very moment, marinating in Jeremiah 31:31–34, Hebrews 8 and 2 Corinthians 3. The eyes of your heart will open to fresh revelation rooted in the bedrock revelation of our faith. Jeremiah is promised a day when God will no longer lead Israel by the hand but will put His law in their minds and hearts. Hebrews tells us that the New Covenant in Jesus is superior to the last one because it is based on "better promises." Paul tells the Corinthians that they are indeed living letters written with the Spirit. In all of these Scriptures, the direct relation of God to His people, actively, of His own volition, is the gracious theme of each.

Our prophetic ears, eyes and mouths must be aligned to our master prophet, Jesus. "The testimony of Jesus is the spirit of prophecy" (Revelation 19:10, NKJV). I want to pause here: Jesus is the centerpiece of prophecy. Prophecy of the future, disclosure of hidden truths—these are meaningless unless Jesus be lifted up. Jesus said, "The words that I speak are spirit and life." Every word that comes from the prophet's mouth must also be spirit and life. They must be the testimony of Jesus. Many prophets today are trying to move in a "call down fire" mentality in imitation of the Hebrew prophets of old, but it will not work. Jesus never called down fire. He had every chance to call down fire, angels or the wrath of His Father, but He did not. Praise God, He did not! He took our wrath and punishment upon Himself. Wrath was exchanged for mercy. Punishment was exchanged for His grace. Our old natures were exchanged for the very life of God pulsating within us.

Prophesying the word of the Lord must come from a New Testament experience with the Father through Jesus the Son. While many go to their own moods, their parents or even one-dimensional pictures of Old Covenant revelation for their image of what God is like, the New Testament tells us that we need look no further than Jesus. "The Son is the radiance of God's glory and the exact representation of his being" (Hebrews 1:3). "In [Jesus] dwells all the fullness of the Godhead bodily" (Colossians 2:9, NKJV). "Anyone who has seen me has seen the Father" (John 14:9). The revelation of God in Christ tears down the idols we have built in our hearts and minds—idols that, if followed, will only bring us to destruction. The images of God we harbor that are sub-Christ are always substandard; they are always more miserly, small-minded, condemning, religious and myopic than the truth. We have a very small vision of Christ. But God wishes to enlarge that vision—to impregnate our hearts with a breathtaking view of His Son.

Jesus is our window into Abba's character and our path to Abba's very being. Jesus said, "I am the way, the truth, and the life. No one comes to the Father except through Me" (John 14:6, NKJV). In order to get to know God, you must know Jesus. In the Bible the word *know* often implies deep intimacy. "Abraham *knew* his wife and they conceived." Over and over this idea of "knowing" someone actually means experiencing union, oneness. We are not just asked to mentally adhere to a set of beliefs about Jesus or to run down a checklist. No! We are invited to perfect union with Him. To be intimate with our Savior. This is the mystery of God, that we are made partakers of Him.

Just as everything that flows from God flows to us through Jesus, He spoke that everything said or done was not of His own will but of His Father's. This means that every prophetic word must go through the mercy, love and grace of Jesus before it reaches the mouth of the yielded New Covenant vessel. If you ever receive a prophetic word that is full of condemnation, judgment or law, it did not go through the saving grace of Jesus. A channel is missing, and the prophetic word is substandard and not worthy of being called a word from the Spirit. Jesus is the Prince of Peace. In His incarnate life, Jesus was anointed "with the Holy Spirit and with power . . . [He] went about doing good and healing all who were oppressed by the devil" (Acts 10:38, NKJV). Jesus reveals a good God. If we prophesy from the heart of Jesus, we will speak like Jesus. The words He spoke were spirit and life. Every time Jesus speaks to people through His vessels, they should always hear the power of life, hope and destiny calling out to them. "For the letter kills, but the Spirit gives life" (2 Corinthians 3:6). If we do not hear "spirit and life" in a prophetic word, we will receive the opposite, which is "flesh and death."

The words of Jesus are powerful and sharp. The Bible says His words are sharper than any two-edged sword, sharp enough to divide between soul and spirit—bone and marrow (see Hebrews 4:12). When Jesus speaks to us, the "sharpness" of the sword does not cut to wound. It cuts between soul (our emotions, thoughts and intentions) and spirit (which is the real us hidden with Christ in God). This division is so minute that it would be like separating the very bone from its inner core of marrow. Only a skilled surgeon should try this. It takes a master cutter! And why does a surgeon operate? In order to heal. In order to save. His words separate, cut and destroy anything that would try to keep us from our divine romance with Him. Remember, Jesus went about doing "good."

He is still in the "doing good" business today. He is our healer forever, and the Spirit of Prophecy is one of the instruments that He uses in that process.

What We Will Unearth

This book is a resource for growing in the knowledge of the prophetic. In the following chapters, we will answer these questions:

- What is prophecy, and what are the gifts of the Spirit? And what is prophecy *not*?
- What does a prophet do (the office of the prophet and the different roles of "seers")?
- What happens when you actually encounter a prophet or the prophetic gift in your life?
- What can we learn from biblical examples of prophets?
- How can you sharpen your discernment, tuning in to the authentic versus phony spiritual power?
- What domino effect is initiated once God's voice speaks to your specific situation and you seize your divine moment?
- What happens when the prophetic word takes a little longer than anticipated to come to pass and you face discouragement?
- How can you be faithful in hearing God in each season of your life (not just the present but the past and the future as well), attuning yourself to the voice you will hear throughout eternity?

Before we begin exploring these areas, let's take a moment to illuminate the basics of prophetic ministry with some helpful definitions[1]:

Prophecy is the "immediate message of God to His people through a divinely anointed utterance." Through prophecy,

---

1. These definitions are adapted from Ernest B. Gentile, *Your Sons and Daughters Shall Prophesy* (Grand Rapids: Chosen Books, 1999), 42–45, 166–67.

God expresses His thoughts and purposes for the current situation. Because it comes "in a flash," without forethought, it is not the same as teaching (which involves research into a subject followed by communication of it). Though prophecy may involve the prediction of future events, it often does not.

A *prophet* is a person authorized to speak for God. The Hebrew word for "prophet" in the Old Testament, *nabi,* is found abundantly in Scripture. One possible origin of this word is a root that means "to bubble forth, to flow"; hence, "to pour forth words."

A *seer* (Hebrew words *roeh* and *hozeh*) is a visionary, one who can "see" into the past, present and future with divine insight. A seer often receives messages in a vision.

A *prophetess* is simply a female prophet. Anna, who gave insight about Jesus when He was just a baby (see Luke 2:36–38), was one of these.

Nabi is by far the most commonly used word for "prophet" in the Hebrew Bible, appearing three hundred times. Only nine men are called "seers" (either *roeh* or *hozeh*), Samuel being the first. *Roeh* and *hozeh* emphasize the mode of *receiving* revelation, that is, seeing in pictures or visions, while *nabi* emphasizes the active work of *declaring* God's word. There may have been little difference scripturally between a prophet and a seer; in 1 Samuel 9:9, we read that "the prophet [*nabi*] of today used to be called a seer [*roeh*]." And yet in 1 Chronicles 29:29, all three words are used for three men: "As for the events of King David's reign, from beginning to end, they are written in the records of Samuel the seer [*roeh*], the records of Nathan the prophet [*nabi*] and the records of Gad the seer [*hozeh*]."

Scripture, of course, is our best resource for learning about the prophetic, because we have the lives of the prophets of those days written for us to learn from. There were many of them; here they are grouped by the times they lived (spellings of the names below come from the King James Version of the Bible).

Era	Comment	Prophets	
Abrahamic prophets		Adam Seth Enos Enoch Methuselah	Noah Shem Salah Eber Melchizedek
Patriarchal prophets	From the Chaldean city of Ur, through Canaan and to Egypt, the nomadic people of the patriarchal period roamed large tracts of the Middle East. This period began with Abraham, included the Exodus and continued to the period of the judges.	Abram Isaac Jacob Joseph Job Caleb Hur Jethro	Moses Aaron Assir Joshua Phinehas Boaz Beor Balaam
Judge-prophets	Following the patriarchal period, Israel evolved into a loose federation of tribes ruled by judges and held together by a common faith and common ancestry. While there were more than twenty judges during this period—Samson being the most infamous—only four were considered to have the status of prophets (two additional judges are included in the list of prophetesses).	Eli Gideon	Elkanah Samuel
Monarchy prophets	The loose federation of Israelite tribes eventually gave way to a monarchy in the best-known period of Israel's history: the kings. The six prophets of the unified kingdom guided Saul, David, Solomon and Rehoboam.	Nathan Gad Ahimelech	Abiathar Shemaiah Iddo
Prophets of Israel	As the monarchy fell apart after the death of King Solomon, the kingdom split into the northern kingdom of Israel, with its ten tribes, and the southern kingdom of Judah, with its two tribes. The northern kingdom was home to nine prophets.	Ahijah Micaiah Beeri Hosea Amos	Jonah Elijah Elisha Oded
Prophets of Judah	The southern kingdom of Judah had the longest list of prophets, 21 in all. Working with good kings and bad, these prophets fought to save Judah from destruction. In the end, though, the Temple was destroyed, Jerusalem came under siege and the Jews were carried away into captivity.	Oded Azariah Hanani Jehu Jahaziel Eliezer Obadiah Joel Zechariah Amoz Isaiah	Zechariah Micah Nahum Maaseiah Neriah Jeremiah Baruch Zephaniah Habakkuk Urijah

Era	Comment	Prophets	
Prophets of the captivity	The destruction of the Temple in Jerusalem was followed by a seventy-year exile that left most of the Jewish population spread throughout Mesopotamia, primarily modern-day Iraq and Iran.	Daniel Ezekiel	Mordecai Seraiah
Prophets of the return	Following the Babylonian captivity, Cyrus decreed that the enslaved Jews were permitted to return to their homelands, rebuild the Temple and reinstitute their religious practices. The five prophets who oversaw that return authored the final portions of the Hebrew Bible.	Ezra Haggai Malach	Nehemiah Zechariah
Prophetesses	The Jewish matriarchs and other prominent holy women make up the prophetesses of the Hebrew Bible. Wives and mothers, most of them, the joy and sorrow of their lives call out to modern readers. We will meet each of them individually in further readings.	Eve Sarai Rebekah Leah Rachel Miriam	Deborah Hannah Abigail Huldah Esther

In the next chapter, we will begin to dissect the "what," "when" and "how" of the prophetic office, the gift of prophecy and the spirit of prophecy. I invite you to dive in experientially to understand firsthand why we need the prophetic in our lives.

3

The Prophetic Office:
The Flow of the Prophet

Life always flows to us when God speaks.
His words are life and spirit.

What Is This Prophets and Prophecy Stuff?

If you are a Christian and the Holy Spirit lives in you, then you have been given the gifts of the Spirit.

The apostle Paul tells us in 1 Corinthians 12:7 that spiritual gifts were given to every believer, but sometimes it seems like our experience tells us otherwise. It is easy to feel that when the Spirit handed out gifts, we were passed by. Or maybe Paul, the great apostle, was also a greater embellisher—maybe he did not actually mean that *every* believer was equipped with the gifts of the Spirit. But what if Paul did not exaggerate? What if we are simply not understanding the Spirit like we should? In order to grow in the prophetic or be used by the Holy Spirit, we need to demystify the process of prophecy and expand our own understanding. Mike Bickle calls this being "supernaturally natural." We see the supernatural part, but we also recognize the natural, physical realm and its influence. This is a powerful recognition that God's ways are miraculous, not ridiculous. His miracles are the morning sun breaking upon a calming sea, a bird in flight or a person functioning beyond themselves—being transformed into something new. These are ordinary miracles.

Over the years in which I have both been a channel for the prophetic and also witnessed numerous brothers and sisters in the Lord operating in such capacity, I have observed something interesting. It seems as though impressions and pictures are the language of the Spirit. Ezekiel saw a spinning wheel, Isaiah saw a multiwinged creature, John saw lamp stands and strangely shaped clouds. In our natural realm, these make no sense, and we are uncomfortable submitting to this. But it requires faith to submit to the way the Spirit speaks. It would be easier if He spoke audibly or showed up in human form. But faith is not about catering to our preferences. It is about yielding to the Spirit. And because His ways are not our ways, it seems He often takes the form of an image or a picture bubbling up into our consciousness.

Like I said, this may sound freaky, but please consider this: God created humankind. He made us to have feelings and thoughts, impressions and emotions. We were made in the image of God. Does it not make sense that He would meet the whole person and interact with the whole person? If the Gospel is true, it has come to the whole person. If the good news is really GOOD NEWS, then it affects all of our being. It heals and restores and saves the soul, the heart, the mind and the body. The power of the prophetic embraces this understanding. There is no realm that the Lord will not invade. One way of saying this is that God loses nothing. When mankind fell—all of him fell. But in Christ, God gets everything back, and then some!

As we begin our journey into defining the different roles the prophetic plays in the Church and throughout the world, I pray that God will begin to download into us a passion and desire to speak for Him—or rather, to allow Him to speak into and through us. Whether we are in grocery stores, Bible studies, airplanes or malls, we must realize that we are His hands, feet and mouth to the world.

Prophets versus Prophecy

The office of the prophet is very different from the gift of prophecy. As I mentioned earlier, the gifts are from the Holy Spirit. The office of the prophet is a governmental function. Like the offices of apostle, evangelist, pastor and teacher, it is an office from Christ—a part or "piece" of Christ, not only a gift. A prophet is the mouthpiece of God to the Body of Christ. He (or she) is not a novice. He does not speak out of his own mind but rather gets a download from the heavens for those people God will bring to him to minister to. He is one who is ordained and called by God; hands were laid on him and he was separated for the office. He is one who is set into the Church by Christ to build up, root up, plant and strengthen. The prophet will disrupt the kingdom of darkness and open the Kingdom doors of heaven so that the King of Glory can come into whatever the prophet is prophesying to. The prophet has the power of decree in his mouth; he will bring a foundation and an establishing of the will of God in the earth. That is the office of the prophet. It rightly has an air of importance, even of intimidation. There is a truly significant aspect to it that must be recognized in the Church. It is built over time. Tested. Approved.

There is no question that a prophet is a spokesman for God. He listens to the very heartbeat of the Father. When prophesying, he conveys the "emotion" the Father is feeling toward an individual, church or nation. When a prophet speaks the words no longer come from himself—it is Jesus the Prophet inside of him speaking. Jesus is the *person* who is speaking. He (Jesus) is the "treasure" in the prophetic vessel's speaking. The Greek word for this is *doma*. It is a *doma* gift. It is not a grace gift. The grace gift of prophecy is a gift that is found in 1 Corinthians 14:1: "Follow after charity, and desire spiritual gifts, but rather that ye may prophesy" (KJV). In

38

contrast, the prophetic office is ordained of God. It is defined by a continued manifestation of prophecies, generally more than just a word of wisdom or a word of knowledge. You can desire prophecy, but you cannot desire the office of the prophet. The office of the prophet is not given but was birthed within the individual before the foundation of the world. Because it is not ordained of man, it cannot be taken away or expire. It is proven over time, confirmed by the Holy Spirit and approved by the Church.

The gift of prophecy, however, is distinctive. By the Spirit of Prophecy, *everyone* can prophesy. The Bible says that the testimony of Jesus is the Spirit of Prophecy. So when the Spirit of Prophecy is in the Church, everyone can prophesy. Young, old, men, women, even the very young—children. Why? The Spirit brings with Him a "prophetic canopy" that causes the atmosphere to become "electric" with the power of prophecy. It opens the door for the people to prophesy. It pulls back the veil to the heavens and causes the people to speak under an open-heaven realm. One way of understanding this is through the mystery of the Trinity. The gift of prophecy is from the Holy Spirit. It is vaporous. Hard to pin down. Evasive. Ever on the move. The office of the prophet is from Jesus Christ Himself. Locatable. Identifiable. At the helm, leading.

The ability to prophesy, which falls on everyone, does not make you a prophet, just as my performing CPR on a person whose heart has stopped does not transform me into a paramedic. A prophet is a person who has come through the ranks or the processes of God, as I will explain below. The life of a prophet is often not an easy life. I remember times in my life when I was spiritually stripped by God to the point that nothing remained but Him. God will shake you from your comfort zone and bring you to the place of trusting Him and Him alone.

In some ways this is because a prophet is one who "bears witness" to leadership and laypeople for his giftings and character. A prophet is a person who has been through the "processes" of God and has come out refined in order that he may be as clear as transparent glass. God wishes others to look at the prophet and see only Him on the other side. This requires an intense and consuming purifying.

Usually, a prophet is a person of God who has been summoned from birth, like Jeremiah. The mantle of the prophet is deposited into the person who is called before the foundation of the world. Ephesians 4:11–13 speaks about the purpose of a prophet. The office of the prophet is to build up, edify and train the Body of Christ. The prophet imparts and brings a manifestation of the Spirit to atmospheres, individuals and even the marketplace. Prophets are not just called to the Body of Christ but also to the world. All through the Word of God, prophets were sent to cities, nations, government officials and individuals. This happens even when it makes them uncomfortable, such as when Jonah would have much rather camped out with his own people than go to those he felt were his enemies or who were beneath him. Prophets have a "bubbling up" of the voice of God deep inside of them. The Word talks about the apostle and prophet being the foundation of the Church (see Ephesians 2:19–20). They are the foundation that strengthens and holds the Church together during the "winter months" of the Church. When the Church is blown by the winds of adversity and is walking through the valley of decision, the foundation must endure by having been built on the revelation of the Lord through the apostles and prophets. The prophet helps, along with the apostle, to build the foundation. So he must be ready to build with no character flaws at all. Thus, when someone is called to be a prophet and continues to walk in the way of the Lord, he has to pass through seasons of development.

"And he gave some, apostles; and some, *prophets;* and some, evangelists; and some, pastors and teachers" (Ephesians 4:11, KJV, emphasis mine). While a lot of people do not understand the office of the prophet, only those who lack knowledge or suffer from unbelief could possibly deny the existence of this precious office today. The prophet brings the Body to maturity, and we do still need to mature. There is little question of that (see Ephesians 4:12–14), although some people may not like to think that a maturation process is needed. But we must open our eyes. If we are perfect or mature, why do we have so many problems such as divorce, gossip and deceit? I do not say this as condemnation. No, the truth is that we will continue to grow until Jesus returns. The prophet's job is to help mature, grow up and strengthen the people for works of service.

The Greek word for prophet is *prophetes*. It means "a foreteller and an inspired speaker of God." This office functions, as do all the offices, completely through the agency of the Holy Spirit, but it is given by Christ Himself. A female prophet is called a prophetess (see Exodus 15:20–21; Judges 4:4–5; 2 Kings 22:14; 2 Chronicles 34:22; Luke 2:36–38). The wife of a prophet is also called a prophetess; Isaiah's wife and Deborah were two of these. We also find prophetesses in the New Testament.

Prophets, like all other ministry offices, have varying degrees of anointing. Some prophets have much stronger anointings than other prophets. The Church has prophets who are called to local churches, cities, governments, states and nations. We see different prophetic anointings in the lives of the prophets Elijah and Elisha. Whatever level of anointing a prophet may have, he or she can increase it through prayer, study and holy living. But each prophet will be called to a specific group of people that God will burn into their heart.

Let's look at the primary qualifications (beyond calling) of the prophet's office, according to Scripture.

The Ministry of the Prophet

The prophet's ministry is mainly one that hears the voice of the Shepherd and shuns the voice of the enemy toward God's people. They bring the *rhema* (illumination) out of the *logos* (written Word) to the people. They speak life into the atmosphere with the power of prophecy, which is the voice of God. This was true with Jesus (see Matthew 9:35; John 4:39), and it was true of the apostle Paul (see 1 Timothy 2:7; 2 Timothy 1:11).

Prophets spend much more time in prayer and study than the average minister. The famed missionary and minister C. T. Studd was once reported as saying that what was needed for a man to speak the word of God was not so much to parse out the meaning and dissect that contextual event, but rather to go into his prayer closet until he was so overflowing with the fire of the Holy Spirit that he had no choice but to speak. Prophets must have an open communication to the heavens with no interference from the enemy. When opposition comes, they must fight the good fight of faith to maintain an open heaven. In the day of Daniel, the prince of Persia came to shut up the heavens, but Daniel prayed to break its power. Prophets must have a prayer life to give to and receive from the Lord. Their messages usually come entirely by inspiration, characterized by a spontaneous flow, once they are in the pulpit. They can behave strangely at times, as well (see Mark 7:33; 8:23; John 9:6). The Lord might call them to do a prophetic act for a person or a church to demonstrate what He is trying to get across to them. Isaiah was instructed to walk around naked for several years in order to get across God's message. Hosea received the instruction to marry and stay married to a known prostitute. Noah was instructed to build the biggest boat that history had ever seen in a place without an ocean, one that had never experienced rain (see Genesis 2:5). The instructions of the Lord can sound like downright insanity sometimes. Yet somehow the unusual behavior always sets someone free.

Theirs is a unique and supernatural ministry indeed. God will take the foolish things of this world to confound the wise. No matter what it takes, at any cost, God will use anything through a prophetic act to get His message across and draw people to Him.

The Revelation Gifts

Prophets also operate very consistently in what have been called the revelation gifts. These are the word of knowledge, the word of wisdom and the discerning of spirits. Prophets see past the ordinary and obvious and into the spirit realm, and they know things about people—past, present and future—but only as the Holy Spirit reveals it to them. They do not know all things about all people at all times. They know only what the Holy Spirit is showing them at the moment. This happens far more consistently with the prophet than with all the other offices. It also happens in private far more often than it does in public (see 1 Kings 17:9–24; 18:1–8; 2 Kings 4:1–37; John 4:5–19).

Before we go further, let's look at definitions and examples of these gifts. They are specifically mentioned in 1 Corinthians 12:7–11:

> Now to each one the manifestation of the Spirit is given for the common good. To one there is given through the Spirit a message of wisdom, to another a message of knowledge by means of the same Spirit, to another faith by the same Spirit, to another gifts of healing by that one Spirit, to another miraculous powers, to another prophecy, to another distinguishing between spirits, to another speaking in different kinds of tongues, and to still another the interpretation of tongues. All these are the work of one and the same Spirit, and he distributes them to each one, just as he determines.

A word of knowledge is generally described as a message from the Holy Spirit for an individual person. It is a definite conviction, impression or knowing that comes to you as an image or a word, a dream or a vision, a phrase of Scripture that is highlighted in your mind. It is often a supernatural understanding of circumstances or problems. It is a "word" from God that serves a purpose for another person, generally by revealing the will or plan of God. It can be about right living and relationships or God-given instructions. It always has to deal with the past or the present, never the future. A word of knowledge is what I received when I prophesied to the man in my congregation. I did not know the circumstances of his situation. But I was given the knowledge of an affair, and I was prompted to speak it out loud.

Similarly, John Wimber, the person often credited as the founder of the Vineyard movement, spoke of a time he walked into a dentist's office, saw the receptionist and knew she was having an affair. He did not know anything else, but then he heard God speak to him, in his spirit, and say the name *Stephen*. He immediately knew this was the name of the man she was seeing. God did not give John any other words or information. John was not looking forward to speaking to this woman, but he knew he had to just say what he was given. He walked up to the desk and said, "Stephen." The woman looked up, wide-eyed. "What did you say?" she whispered fiercely.

He repeated the name.

The woman then appeared to be scared and said, "Who told you to say that?" To which John smiled, shrugging slightly, and, embarrassed, mumbled, "God."

"I knew it!" the woman cried as she broke down with the revelation of the truth.

The word of knowledge is not often or always a full revelation. It can be portions of a situation or phrase, but this is so that you are given just enough to carry out God's directions. After all, the revelation is not about you, nor is it coming from yourself. If it made complete sense to you, then it would not feel much like faith or trust in God, would it?

John Hamel, another teacher of the spiritual gifts, tells this small story of his experience with a word of knowledge:

> Possibly the smallest Word of Knowledge I know is as follows. One day my dump truck refused to start. I said, "Father, what's wrong with that truck?" Immediately, on the inside of my spirit, I saw a picture. It was the coil on my dump truck. I could see right through it. There was a bead of water inside of it. It was hindering the proper flow of electricity.
>
> I went outside and stuck the rolled up tip of a paper towel into the coil. It became saturated, wicking the water up into it. I jumped inside the truck, turned the key and the engine fired up immediately. I was a baby Christian and that completely blew my mind. You can believe that I shouted praises. My dump truck mattered to God because my dump truck mattered to me and I matter to God.

Second is the word of wisdom. The gift of a word of wisdom has to do with directions and behaviors. It is the wisdom of God given to your spirit so that you can understand what to do or what to say.

It is not a direction that can be ascertained just through Scripture quotations. It is a direct revelation of wisdom from God, through your neural network and into your mind. It will speak to specific situations and it always speaks to the future. This is the biggest difference between a word of knowledge and a word of wisdom.

Another one of John Hamel's stories that helped me understand this involves a substantial sum of money. A man was offering him a check for thousands of dollars in order to attend Bible college. Yet John had an uneasy feeling about it. So he prayed about it and received a word of wisdom. He heard God telling him it was not time to go to school. John asked Him when, and he heard, *In nine months*.

John refused the man's generous offer, though he had no natural reason to do so. And yet in nine month's time, a supernatural orchestration of events showed that it was now the season for John to go to school. And the Lord provided for it through several other offers.

This is an example of a word of wisdom, as it had to do with a future event. It was a revelation of information that had a specific purpose for later on. Yet it was given to John so that he would know what to do in that moment, as well as in the future. It was direction and leading, a mapping out of God's will.

Third is the discerning of spirits. Hamel writes, "I should immediately point out that this Gift is not called the 'Gift of Discernment.' Some use this erroneous name. We should call this Gift what the Bible calls it. The Bible calls it the 'Discerning of Spirits.'" Also, I want to be very clear: This is not the "gift of criticism." Some meddling individuals are always sticking their noses in the business of others, claiming, "I have the gift of discernment. I just want to help." These folks actually have a critical spirit. I heard one person say they had "the gift of pot-stirring," and essentially they meant this same thing. I promptly replied that if I were they I might read up on the gifts again and see where exactly "pot-stirring" or "critiquing" were in Scripture.

The discerning of spirits is a supernatural revelation from the Spirit of God that opens one's eyes to the activities of the spirit realm. Through the operation of this gift, one can see Jesus, the Holy Spirit, the similitude of God, angels, Satan, demons and any other spiritual beings, objects or activities. This gift also enables the possessor to discern the power, good or evil, that prompts certain behaviors in other living beings (see Numbers 22:27–35; Mark 8:33; John 1:47; 6:70).

Any time an individual experiences a Holy Spirit–induced inward vision, open vision, trance or dream allowing that person to peer into the spirit realm, the discerning of spirits is in operation. In fact it is absolutely imperative that this be the case.

A friend of mine grew up in a church that, like many others, denied the existence of modern-day prophecy and other such gifts of the Spirit. Naturally, she approached prophetic gatherings and Spirit-led meetings with great skepticism, if not criticism.

You may have heard it said that "God is a gentleman. He will never force Himself on you." It is true. If you are not looking for the gifts of the Spirit—if you are not willing to receive them—He will not give them. He will not waste His gift on someone who will reject it. This is why most critics of the prophetic and the gifts of the Spirit never change their minds; they are not willing to learn any different. You cannot receive into your hands what God desires to give when they are tightly clenched.

My friend was at a gathering of several hundred believers to listen to a special speaker. After a lengthy time of singing, she was feeling tired in her spirit. All the people around her were dancing and waving their arms, deeply involved in seeking the spiritual realm. My friend, Elizabeth, was frustrated with the emotionality of the moment. To avoid greater frustration and to separate herself from the experience, she got up to leave the room, but she decided to stand in the very back of the sanctuary, next to the double doors.

As soon as the speaker got up to preach, he started leading the group in prayer, asking for the Holy Spirit to fill the room. Quickly, the atmosphere in the room—even the sounds of the room—changed. From her vantage point in the back of the room, Elizabeth saw the several hundred attendees simultaneously fall on their knees. Still holding on to her skepticism, Elizabeth remained standing against the doors, the last one in the room not bowing.

A moment later, a quickening came over Elizabeth. She felt the presence of the Spirit on her, and she knew she was not alone. She heard a voice in her heart gently but clearly say, *Elizabeth, this is My Spirit.*

She immediately knew the phenomenon was from the Lord, and she did not question its validity. She knew intrinsically it was the Spirit of the Lord as she let her knees bend to the floor. "Far be it from me to stand against You," she said as she joined the rest of the group on the floor. God overwhelmed my friend's senses. He leveled her carefully erected walls, but only as she opened up and allowed Him in.

This is a specific example of the discerning of spirits. Often it is hard to tell whether something is man-made or from God, or even from an evil spirit. This can cause us to put up walls or defenses and to be critical of spiritual experiences. We are accustomed to, and have been inundated with, so many sad stories that we constantly expect them to recur right in front of us. We are primed to witness the absolute worst. Needless to say, we are cautious. This is not necessarily bad—we should be careful what we submit to. But for Elizabeth, it was clear that the spirit involved was the Spirit of Christ, the same Spirit that already dwelled within her.

Prophets experience *visions* as well as revelations (see 2 Corinthians 12:1). Prophets are not omniscient, but they *do* have visions and revelations far more than the average minister or layperson (see 2 Kings 4:27; 5:20–27). This is not the prophet's main job, though. He or she is first and foremost a vessel that flows with the voice of God. When the Holy Spirit does reveal something to the prophet, it is to be judged according to biblical standards by other prophets and the congregation (see 1 Corinthians 14:29–30). The revelations are to be weighed in accordance with God's Word and the person of Jesus.

The prophet's ministry is also a *healing* ministry. The prophet cannot heal just anyone they will; there is, however, a consistent healing anointing that accompanies this office (see 2 Kings 5:1–14;

Matthew 14:36; Luke 4:27; 17:11–19; John 9:6–7). Some prophets operate more strongly in revelation gifts than in the gifts of healing, and vice versa. It is up to the Holy Spirit which prophet will operate more strongly in what gifts and when.

Prophets can also give direction and guidance for people, businesses and ministries. In the Old and New Testaments prophets gave guidance to kings, priests and common people. They can bring confirmation and revelation to circumstances or situations a person might be going through. Think of the prophet as a life coach, but with different and divine insight. Prophets bring clarity and calm as they listen to the Holy Spirit.

Stirring the Waters

Many times, when people begin to seek out prophecy, it means that they have a definite call to prophesy. This is the first telltale sign of the hand of God on their lives. Whatever you are seeking, that same thing is seeking you. It stirs up the "law of attraction." It is like a magnet; it is deep calling unto deep. The deep of God is calling, stirring up and pulling out the deep in you.

There is a well of salvation deep inside every Christian that the Father seeks to "stir up." Just like the pool of Bethesda that was said to be stirred up by the will of God, the waters begin to stir up in you like a tidal wave, calling you to open your mouth so the message can come out. You feel a burden to prophesy. It is far greater than a desire. It is a compulsion. You could not generate it if you wanted to. It is more of a weight than anything else. You feel a burden to seek out spiritual things. You are not satisfied just being a good, churchgoing, nominal Christian. You are not satisfied being a person of witness or a person who can lay hands on the sick. The "motor" of the Spirit in you begins to turn and burn a fire that cannot be quenched! Inside, you are motivated to speak into the lives of people to bring change and order. It is time to desire spiritual gifts! We must go higher, further and deeper into the Spirit. As Jesus did with Simon Peter out on the lake, the Lord is calling us to walk on the waters of the Spirit. Are you hungry for more than what religion has been feeding you? Here is a radical question: Could it be the Lord directed you to purchase this book because He wants to open you up and satisfy your craving for more? The same voice of God that called John in the book of Revelation to "come up hither" is the same voice calling you to break open the heavens and come before the throne of the Lord with boldness to ask what you will! Your destiny is calling you. Can you hear it through the noise of negativity, criticism, caution and outright fear?

This "burning" or "burden" or "compulsion" does not have a specific name. But it is known to many as an "unction." When that "unction" comes upon you, it can become resident in you. You begin to seek it, ask for it and knock at it. It draws you into its orbit because it is already inside of you. Jesus said He was the door in John 10:9. You have to begin to "open the door," which is Christ in you, the hope of glory. Jesus the Prophet is inside of you. He has to grow into full bloom. When the desire comes, you will begin to seek Him, and you will be filled with the fullness of what He has planned for your life with that gifting. There is a door in each person that God desires to open! The Word talks about doors, keys, openings and closings. He has given you the keys to bind and loose! Use your keys to open up the door of your spirit and release the anointing of Christ so He will have His way in you. Allow Him to work through you both the willing and the doing of His pleasure.

> For what we preach is not ourselves, but Jesus Christ as Lord, and ourselves as your servants for Jesus' sake. For God, who said, "Let light shine out of darkness," made his light shine in our hearts to give us the light of the knowledge of God's glory displayed in the face of Christ. But we have this treasure in jars of clay to show that this all-surpassing power is from God and not from us.
>
> 2 Corinthians 4:5–7

There is a treasure in these earthen vessels. Discover and unlock the treasure in you!

Going Back to School

A prophet develops in the school of the prophets—in the company of other like-minded and clean-hearted men and women. Instruction will discipline you, mature you and open up the door for wisdom to flood into you to prepare you for your destiny. This will probably be the first time that you realize God is showing you something about somebody. God speaks to you in pictures, in visions, in dreams and even through art. When you come before the prophet and you receive a prophetic word, it is Jesus who is speaking to you. The person of Jesus Christ manifests Himself as the master Prophet in the person giving the prophetic word. "People look at the outward appearance, but the LORD looks at the heart" (1 Samuel 16:7).

Prophets have the "eye of the eagle"; they must see through the eye of God and not through the eye of man. You have to see the way God sees, understanding that it is the prophet Jesus who is speaking and not the vessel. But it comes pouring out of an earthen vessel, so prophecy must be judged by other prophets according to Scripture. The Bible says, "Despise not prophesyings. Prove all things; hold fast that which is good" (1 Thessalonians 5:20–21, KJV). Why would Paul feel a need to advise a church not to despise prophecy? Perhaps there are many reasons, but one that feels applicable in light of what I have seen over the years is that it is easy to hear a glorious truth out of a cracked vessel and discount the truth. This is why our attention is turned to proving what is being said. Leave the vessel to the Lord. Allow God to refine His channel for speaking. But take to heart what is being said. Prove it. Weigh it. Do not despise it.

Still, why must it be judged? Because the vessel is not perfect, and New Testament prophecies are not on the same level as Old Testament prophecies. The prophet can miss what God is saying. He shows a picture in the prophet's mind or grabs his imagination with an image, and now the prophet has to communicate what he saw to the person. God uses your intellect, what you have learned, what you have known and your experiences as you have grown to communicate the things you see. Remember, He is using an earthen vessel. So He will use *your* vocabulary to minister to the individual that you are prophesying to.

God might show you a flower; immediately the understanding of a flower comes to you, and now you must communicate what that means. Always say only what God tells you to say. Sometimes in the prophetic, we tend to "explain" or try to "figure out" what God is saying, and we lose the main content He desires to convey to the individual. Speak what He speaks and hush when He hushes—this is my motto. Obedience is better than sacrifice. Do not add to or take away from the "word" of God. If God shows you a flower, say "God showed me a flower." Do not feel the need to add on to the miraculous occasion of God giving you insight or a vision.

The prophet must develop a sense of prophetic timing. Timing is very important when speaking for God. Not everything that is right is necessarily for right now; thus you must submit your entire self to the Lord in order to discern His timing. Your entire being becomes an instrument for God's use; you are the "property of God." God can speak to you by impressions, pictures, dreams, visions or even through natural happenings to relate His message. When He triggers what is inside of you, you begin to speak. It will begin to "boil up" like fire, and His anointing pours oil on that prophetic word. It is time for the word to be delivered! You might look at a person and feel a sensation coming over your body. What God is doing is visiting that which is in the person's body onto you so that you can recognize and name it. His hand is calling you to bring healing to the person. Some are His hands, some are His feet; *you* are His voice! So allow God to use your voice when He begins to speak words of life, hope and peace to people through you, His vessel.

Laying Foundations

Prophets are foundation-layers in the building up of the Church. Often, they have a rough job. Many desire to be prophets and find out the job is not all it is cracked up to be. They are hated by the religious system, the Pharisees, Sadducees and even some Spirit-filled people who sit beside them in church. Not everyone desires to hear what God really wants to say to them, but prophets must be faithful to speak when He says to speak to "whosoever." A foundation ministry is not really the glorified ministry it appears to be. We walk upon foundations, we spit on foundations and we disregard foundations. Most accurately we rarely notice the stones we are stepping on. They are an unnoticed and obscure reality.

If you are called to be a prophet, then, it means you will have to walk through some rough times, because foundations go through roughness. You must be strong in the Lord and the power of His might. You will encounter all kinds of persecutions: people lying about you, people discrediting your word, people not trusting you and people turning away from you. If Judas could turn his back on Jesus, then people will turn their backs on you, as well. Religion hates the prophetic! A prophet's enemy is always religion, because it will try to confine you to your comfort zone and will never release you to "Come up hither" to hear more from the Lord. Religion is terrified of being exposed, scared to death of being found out as a tired husk waiting to be thrown to the rubbish heap. And so it will do just about anything to protect itself from exposure, including destroying you. A surefire way to minimize this is to always keep yourself surrounded by those who are "water walkers," people who never settle for things that are comfortable, who always desire to go "from glory to glory and from faith to faith."

Always remember that your ministry as a foundation-layer will require you to get the freshness of heaven—the creativity of the Kingdom and the witty inventions of the Spirit. Foundations are not always built the same way. You are called, as a prophet, to get a specific word for a specific person. Think of being a messenger; your job is to deliver the message with as much accuracy and efficiency as possible. But the experience is inconsistent. Today's message will not necessarily come the same way as yesterday's. Some people will love the word of the Lord that you give them, and some will not. It is not about the eloquence of our speech, but it is about being a foundation-layer.

We must realize it is not an easy job to be a prophet. Prophets are called to lay foundations in the Spirit long before others even see it. What happens when a big chain store decides to expand to a territory where it was not invited because the city did not desire to "stretch its tent" and grow? Sometimes it takes years after the new store takes root for others to recognize the new jobs and revenue that came to the city because of that new store. You will never be liked when the Lord uses you to pull up the pegs from someone's tent and command its borders to increase and grow. Change is an evil word to many. But in the long run, when the veil is removed from their eyes and they see all that is out there for them, they will be thankful you spoke that change.

Training in Rejection

Jesus came as a prophet, but the Bible says He was despised and rejected of men. So as a prophet, you can count on being despised and rejected of men because you are God's mouthpiece. The greater the rejection, the greater the anointing—and you are in good company! Because you are rejected, you are in the same boat with Jesus, who said that the disciple is not above his master. If they rejected Jesus the Prophet, they will reject you.

In essence, they are still rejecting Jesus the Prophet because He is speaking through you. People reject foundation ministry, but they love the "tickling of the ears" ministry. Do not ever look at people's faces when you are prophesying; just look at His face to hear what He is saying to them. I rarely hear people approach a minister to say, "Thank you for that thing you said that I completely disagree with and am really wrestling about." Instead most people say, "Thank you so much—I loved what you said!" They loved it because they agreed with it, because it mirrored their own psyche. For a prophet, it is different. If you are doing your job, you can count on upset feelings somewhere. The reason for this is always the same: God has spoken to them, His hand weighs on them—and they would rather He (and He through you) shut up.

If you do not see yourself the way God sees you—whether your flawed perspective is as inferior or self-exalting—you cannot walk worthy of your vocation. So I ask: What seest thou? We must have a revelation of who we really are in Christ and who Christ really is in us. We must allow the Father to heal us from anything that might come back to haunt us or be a stumbling block in our lives or ministry.

You see, God has given a certain measure of authority and dominion to the prophetic ministry. That measure of authority differs based on callings and maturity, but generally speaking it is the authority to speak forth the word of the Lord boldly. The Bible says, "The righteous are as bold as a lion" (Proverbs 28:1). With a roar in our mouths, we have the authority to root out, destroy and throw down spiritual opposition; authority to build the Church of Jesus Christ; authority to plant seeds of the Kingdom of God in the earth. Walking in that authority requires courage to face all that stands in the way of the will of God. Prophets are called to "prepare the way for the Lord" (Luke 3:4).

On the other hand, we must also walk in humility, with utter dependence on God. We do not have authority to utter prophecies without an unction. We do not have authority to be judgmental and critical of others just because we have exercised our senses to discern good and evil. We do not have authority to question how or when God decides to move. That is not our place. How dare we imagine it is. These are some of the areas that lead us into the deception of seeing ourselves high and lifted up, instead of humbly acknowledging Jesus as the supreme authority and trusting Him in all things.

Even John the Baptist, the one Jesus described as more eminent and remarkable than any other prophet, had to struggle with this. Herod had put John in prison, where he awaited his execution. Doubtless he was a little distressed by the prospect of his head soon being delivered on a silver platter to a manipulative woman with an ax to grind (see Matthew 14:3–11). Hello, Jezebel spirit! The Jezebel spirit will always want the prophets of God silenced and cut off. It pursues its priorities at the expense of God's foundation-layers. John probably heard about how Jesus was setting the captives free. The devil may have whispered in his imagination, "Jesus could come to your rescue, but He is hanging you out to dry." John sent his disciples to Jesus with a question: "Are You the Messiah, or should we wait for another?"

John was not questioning whether Jesus was the Son of God. Rather, he was questioning why Jesus would not come to his rescue—and he seemed a little irritated about it. Jesus' reply was interesting: He gave John's disciples the message that the blind could see, the lame could walk, lepers were cleansed, the deaf heard, the dead were raised up and the poor had the Gospel preached to them (see Matthew 11:4–5).

If someone rejects your ministry, you cannot wear your feelings on your sleeve. A foundational stone is in the foundation, not the tower. Foundation stones are abused. There will be those who will mock you, make fun of you, call you a heretic or just plain not like you. You must find your identity not in man's validation but in God and God alone. What can man do to such a one as this? If the mantle of prophet is on you, you are going to be abused and hurt and even have your best friend betray you—like Jesus the Prophet. That is the road carved out for you. I heard one old church worker say, "Anyone living by the life of God can expect to have their journey pass through Golgotha." This is true of every Christian living by God's Spirit, but it is especially true of those whom He has called to build up others.

God's people are "built on the foundation of the apostles and prophets, with Christ Jesus himself as the chief cornerstone" (Ephesians 2:20). The training of a prophet tends to be rough and hard; any reflection on the Old Testament prophets will reveal this. Death threats, illnesses and other physical or emotional suffering were common trials for an Old Testament prophet. If there are cracks in the foundation, the building will be shaky. Character must be developed, emotions must be stable and integrity must be the cry of your heart. More weight and pressure on a foundation will eventually cause cracks to open, and the building will collapse. If there are cracks in your vessel, or if there are cracks in your life, God has to take you through some difficult experiences to heal those cracks. Then you will be able to stand as you are called—to be a builder and a foundation in the Kingdom of God.

Refining the Prophet

Much more goes into the making of a prophet. There is the periodic humiliation (believe me when I say a resounding, "Ouch"). God asked Isaiah, for example, to walk around naked for three years (see Isaiah 20:2–3). Continual sanctification, devotion to the Word of God (you cannot prophesy beyond your knowledge of God's Word) and of course intimacy with God are vital in the prophet's journey. Amos 3:7 is a popular Scripture for prophetic ministry, and it is true: "Surely the Sovereign Lord does nothing without revealing his plan to his servants the prophets." God does tell His secrets to His prophets. But He will not share His heart with blabbermouths or those who do not spend enough time with Him to listen to what is on His mind, because He will not throw His pearls before swine.

Accountability is one of the absolute essentials for prophetic maturity. Every prophet, old or young, must take responsibility for his or her actions. Where is the character and integrity in prophetic ministry today? "A good name is rather to be chosen" (Proverbs 22:1, KJV). Let's face it, no prophet is perfect. Any prophet can miss it from time to time; that is why all prophecy should be judged. It goes back to humility. Mature prophets will humbly admit their errors and seek the Lord's face for revelation about why they made them. Do not be afraid to admit, "I missed it." Learn from your mistakes and go on. An old saying goes, "If you do not learn from your mistakes, you will be destined to repeat them." If you have breath in your body, you will make mistakes in this life. Repent and go on. Forgiveness is the great tool of Jesus that He gave us at Calvary. Use it—it will literally save your life.

Local leaders can guide the spiritual growth and maturing of the saints who show interest in the gifts of the Holy Spirit. Signs of prophetic maturation should be evident before a prophet is allowed to operate publicly. Many prophets will fight against such rules or guidelines, but this type of response is evidence of a lack of maturity. That means it is back to the Potter's house for another season of breaking.

Senior prophets must give a budding prophet boundaries. He must be proven before he can move in other areas. If he is not, he can release all kinds of negative things in people's lives. He can speak some things out of season. At times when God gives you a word, you cannot release the word at that time. You have to wait for the right season. Proper timing of the Lord is everything! Only God knows the answer to the "when" and the "where." Just be patient and wait on the Lord for clarity and timing.

If you are a prophet, then you are a servant. And a servant does not have any rights. They have relinquished their rights in order to be available for their Master, who tells them to do this and that. You are a servant of the Lord. If you are not a senior prophet, that makes you a servant of your leader or pastor. Elisha was a servant of Elijah; remember that great servants become great leaders. Serve and then lead; that way when you lead, you can serve. We serve the vision of another in order for God and the congregation to confirm that we are worthy of carrying vision at all.

The person a prophet will prophesy to is not necessarily the same person in whom the will of God is fulfilled. God spoke His will to Abram, saying, "Get out of your country, and I will show you a new land." But His will was fulfilled in Abraham. God spoke to Jacob, and His will was fulfilled in Israel. His name changed to reflect his new nature. When God speaks a word and reveals His will to you, He has to take you through training.

The first mention of the word *prophet* in Scripture is connected to the prayer life of the prophet (see Genesis 20:7). That prophet was Abraham, and he was a man of prayer. He was also a man of faith, which is why he is called the father of the faithful. We develop faith in direct correlation with the time we are willing to

57

spend on our faces before our Father God. All prophets must have a prayer life. Prayer is also a prophetic anointing.

When you begin to pray, you are having a conversation with God. When you can hear what He is saying, you will begin to develop your prophetic ministry. As you come to know the voice of God in prayer, the people who hear you prophesy will say, "I know this is God." Your prophetic word will only be accurate and properly seasoned if you become a man or woman of prayer. Your prophetic words develop along with your relationship with God. If you are my friend and I talk to you every day, you are going to know about me. I am going to know about you, also, because an exchange takes place. There is a relationship.

In prayer, God is exchanging Himself *into* you. He is giving an interpretation of Himself in every area of your life. If you are called to the office of the prophet, you must be a man or woman of prayer. Prayer brings revelation of the I AM because He shares Himself with who I am. I know what He is saying because we have a relationship. You must learn to lock yourself up at the throne of God and throw away the key. Get in front of the Most High and allow everything else to melt away—your distractions, your failures, your sin, your self—until the two become one. Learn to be "bone of His bone" and "flesh of His flesh" by being intimate with Him. The Scripture tells us "to know Him." As we said earlier, if you look at the word *know* in Genesis, you will see it is like when Adam "knew" Eve. It means knowing someone intimately. Prophets must know the heartbeat of Jesus. You must become like the apostle John, whom Jesus called "the beloved." Learn to lay your head upon the chest of Jesus to hear His heartbeat. As a prophet, you must know and hear what His heart is saying. You must have a lifestyle of prayer. The prophetic and prayer go hand in hand.

A prophet's ministry includes edification, exhortation and comfort. It also moves in the elements of prediction, foretelling, guidance, rebuking and judgment. When a person is operating in the gift of prophecy and only prophesies exhortation, comfort and edification, that person is operating under a grace gift. You can know it by hearing the delivery.

An exhortation coaches people through the "dos" and "don'ts" of following the Lord. It helps them know what is going to happen if they do this or do not do that. Edification is for building up and ministering comfort. Many of you, when you heard God speak to you through a prophet, began to cry because you heard something that you knew was from God. Sometimes a seasoned prophet brings correction. If he sees something out of order in your life, he will not speak it to destroy you. He will speak it to edify you. Your spirit knows what the prophet is saying.

A seasoned prophet has to know how to use the knife of a surgeon over the knife of a butcher. Anyone can be a butcher, but a surgeon is a skilled person. If you are called to the office of the prophet, you are called to be a skilled surgeon.

Prophets often functioned as seers (see Numbers 12:6; Hosea 12:10). Samuel, for example, was first called a seer before he was called a prophet. A seer is a person who has a receptive ministry in the prophetic realm. A seer receives information. He acts as an advisor. Every senior prophet must have a seer or seers around him; because he is focused ahead, he cannot see behind himself. A seer is just that, one who sees. They are on the lookout, ever alert to what God is doing.

You cannot drive a car while looking in the rearview mirror or you will crash. Seers look in the rearview mirror for you. When senior prophets separate and ordain seers in their house, the seers receive an impartation of the leader's spirit. They will be synchronized to the leader and his vision.

A prophet is a watchman. Prophets operate in the ministry of helps. Some people are called to be prophets, but they do not want to operate in the ministry of helps. They do not want to clean the bathroom, sweep the floors, carry out the garbage or lift the pastor's bag. If you are called to be a prophet, operate in the ministry of helps. You are never above serving your church or others. This is where your ministry will develop, because your anointing is to "go." Your anointing is not to stay, saying, "Let me pray all day and get visions and dreams." You do not develop like that. As you go, you develop. As you begin to walk out your ministry, you develop. The men whom

Jesus developed to be apostles served Him. They were ushers. If you do not know how to seat people in an orderly fashion, how will you know how to give a word to bring order into people's lives?

Operate in whatever area of ministry your pastor places you, even if you do not understand what God is doing, for you are in training. Obey those who are your authorities, who have rule over you. You may have received prophetic words that you are going to be a "ruler in the house of God." What if the pastor or a deacon says, "Brother, help us with these chairs"? Will you say, "What chairs? I'm called to be a ruler in the house of God. You've missed God! That's not *my* assignment"? Assisting them is developing you. Whatever stage you are in is part of your development—it is part of your preparation.

Prophets, we have to trust God. We have to trust that He has given us authority. We have to trust those in authority over us. We have to trust that we are who He says we are. We have to trust that He will give us the right prophetic words to say to the right people at the right time. We have to be humble enough to trust Him with our lives and ministries, just as Jeremiah did. The alternative is clear: If we stumble in distrust, we cannot see the truth.

A Prophet Helps Perfect the Church

> And He gave some to be apostles, and some prophets, and some evangelists, and some pastors and teachers, for the perfecting of the saints for the work of the ministry, and for the edifying of the body of Christ, until we all come into the unity of the faith and of the knowledge of the Son of God, unto a perfect man, unto the measure of the stature of the fullness of Christ; that we henceforth be no longer children, tossed to and fro and carried about with every wind of doctrine by the sleight of men and their cunning and craftiness, whereby they lie in wait to deceive.
>
> Ephesians 4:11–14 (KJ21)

If someone says that the office of the prophet is not for today, know that they are in error—and usually serving an agenda behind that error. God gave the fivefold ministry, the apostle, prophet, evangelist, pastor and teacher, to the Body of Christ until He returns to bring His Kingdom to earth. If the office of the prophet is not for today, then neither are the offices of the pastor, evangelist, teacher or apostle. Ephesians clearly shows that the office of the prophet is for today. God is raising up the prophets again to bring order and direction to the Church. The truth behind what God is doing is that God is interested in restoring His Church. The prophet and apostle were the first two offices given to the Body of Christ, according to Ephesians 2:20. So today they will be the last offices to be restored to full authority, power and dominion before Christ returns.

Prophets are so vital to the health of New Testament churches that Luke spared no expense in chronicling their impact so all future generations of believers could draw from this reliable Spirit-inspired historic record when setting in place the structure of local churches in every city and nation. The Church of Jesus Christ cannot and will not truly function without this order, which has been set before us so we can follow in building "His" local church. He said, "I will build *My* Church, and the gates of hell will not prevail against it." The reason why we have not seen power today like that seen in the book of Acts is because we have not obeyed His pattern to help structure and equip the Church of Jesus Christ. She is "built on the foundation of the apostles and prophets, with Christ Jesus himself as the chief cornerstone" (Ephesians 2:20). Without the apostles and prophets as the foundation or concrete of a church, it is merely a building full of people. The Word says, "To obey is better than sacrifice" (1 Samuel 15:22). Do not build your church on sand (lack of stability or foundation). Build it on the solid rock (revelation or fullness) of Christ. Prophets and apostles will always bring fresh revelation (manna) from the throne of God to the local body. Without revelation, we will simply be eating stale bread. Prophets will always bring forth revelation and impartation. This is why the Lord told us to pray, "Give us this day our daily bread" (revelation). Stale bread will always produce mold in the Church.

What Scripture Teaches about Prophets

The following is a list of roles played by prophets throughout Scripture. In later chapters of this book, we will discuss some practical ways that these roles function today.

- Prophets prophesy to kings and governmental authorities: "But the prophet Gad said to David, 'Do not stay in the stronghold. Go into the land of Judah.' So David left and went to the forest of Hereth" (1 Samuel 22:5).
- Prophets anoint kings and leaders: "There have Zadok the priest and Nathan the prophet anoint him king over Israel. Blow the trumpet and shout, 'Long live King Solomon!'" (1 Kings 1:34).
- Prophets have healing abilities: "She said to her mistress, 'If only my master would see the prophet who is in Samaria! He would cure him of his leprosy'" (2 Kings 5:3).
- Prophets preach and teach the word of the Lord:

  > So the elders of the Jews continued to build and prosper under the preaching of Haggai the prophet and Zechariah, a descendant of Iddo. They finished building the temple according to the command of the God of Israel and the decrees of Cyrus, Darius and Artaxerxes, kings of Persia.
  >
  > Ezra 6:14

- Prophets are called to go to the nations of the earth: "Before I formed you in the womb I knew [or chose] you, before you were born I set you apart; I appointed you as a prophet to the nations" (Jeremiah 1:5).
- Prophets prepare the way of the Lord: "This is he who was spoken of through the prophet Isaiah: 'A voice of one calling in the wilderness, "Prepare the way for the Lord, make straight paths for him"'" (Matthew 3:3).
- Prophets reveal secrets: "'Sir,' the woman said, 'I can see that you are a prophet'" (John 4:19). The woman at the well

perceived Jesus to be a prophet because He revealed the truth about her husbands.

- Prophets perform miraculous signs: "After the people saw the sign Jesus performed, they began to say, 'Surely this is the Prophet who is to come into the world'" (John 6:14).

4

Prophetic Roles for the Prophet!

*The prophetic word brings change. Do not ask the Lord to
speak to you unless you are ready.*

What Does a Prophet Do?

The book of Acts is a historical record of the words and actions of
the early Church—perhaps the most exciting time in Church history, when believers were learning what they were capable of after
the Resurrection. We will look at this book closely for examples
of the prophetic at work.

Right away, chapter 2 clearly illustrates how prophets and prophecy are used to reveal, confirm, predict, commission, guide, warn
and demonstrate. Over 120 disciples were gathered in one room
when suddenly the Holy Spirit filled the house and their bodies and
they began to speak in more than a dozen foreign languages by the
unction of the Holy Spirit at Pentecost—a prophetic manifestation that helped to prepare the hearts of the people and confirm
the apostle Peter's Gospel message, bringing 3,000 new believers
into the Kingdom.

Like many believers today, the apostle Paul had his ministry confirmed by a prophetic revelation. The Lord confronted Paul on the road to Damascus and told him he would receive further word there. When Paul arrived, a man named Ananias came to see him. Paul tells of his encounter with the prophet in Acts 22:

> He was a devout observer of the law and highly respected by all the Jews living there. He stood beside me and said, "Brother Saul, receive your sight!" And at that very moment I was able to see him.
>
> Then he said: "The God of our ancestors has chosen you to know his will and to see the Righteous One and to hear words from his mouth. You will be his witness to all people of what you have seen and heard. And now what are you waiting for? Get up, be baptized and wash your sins away, calling on his name."
>
> Acts 22:12–16

After this time, Saul was renamed Paul, and he committed himself to spreading the news of Jesus to the rest of the Jews. In Acts 13, the church in Antioch was busy worshiping and fasting. It is during this time that they received a word of wisdom. The text reads,

> Now in the church at Antioch there were prophets and teachers: Barnabas, Simeon called Niger, Lucius of Cyrene, Manaen (who had been brought up with Herod the tetrarch) and Saul. *While they were worshiping the Lord and fasting,* the Holy Spirit said, "Set apart for me Barnabas and Saul for the work to which I have called them." So after they had fasted and prayed, they placed their hands on them and sent them off.
>
> Acts 13:1–3, emphasis added

After Paul was called, he was commissioned with Barnabas to preach the Gospel. This reveals that there is a time between the calling and commissioning of a prophet, and it also demonstrates the pattern for being sent out to do the work of ministry. It also demonstrates how a gift of knowledge was given through and during a time of worshiping and fasting. Remember, the Lord wants to reveal Himself and His words to His children. It is our choice to enter into conversation with Him.

The prophetic ability to predict events or circumstances is also recorded in Scripture.

> During this time some prophets came down from Jerusalem to Antioch. One of them, named Agabus, stood up and through the Spirit predicted that a severe famine would spread over the entire Roman world. (This happened during the reign of Claudius.) The disciples, as each one was able, decided to provide help for the brothers and sisters living in Judea. This they did, sending their gift to the elders by Barnabas and Saul.
>
> Acts 11:27–30

Because of Agabus's testimony, or word of wisdom, suffering was avoided and lives were spared. This is the fruit of prophecy— always bringing about the plans of God, especially when it comes to extending mercy and grace that will save the souls of men.

Pastors and Prophets Are a Team

We have examined what prophets do, but what does that look like in a communal context? How do prophets coexist and function in the world? Do they roam wild and hide in secret places, only speaking words when God flies them into a group of people? Are they spontaneous, fly-by-the-seat-of-their-pants kind of people born with roller skates on their feet? Or are prophets within our communities, within our local churches, rubbing shoulders with our friends and families? Are they locatable, visible and actual?

Obviously, they are the latter. Most of a prophet's interactions will coincide with a pastor's. This is logical since pastors lead and teach their congregations in the Word of God. But they are not the same thing, pastors and prophets. They are similar in leadership influence but different in functioning.

The pastoral role functions on a totally different realm from that of the prophet. It does not mean either one is more important than the other. It simply means they each have their place in the Church to do what they are called to do. One will guide and direct and the other will shepherd and protect. The pastoral ministry is to take care of the flock. He takes care of and provides food for the sheep. A pastor cannot bring the direction that a prophet brings. He can help, but he does not have a foundation ministry. He does not know the foundational stones. He may put you in one area just to have the prophet say, "God said to put you over here."

Conflict arises between a pastor and a prophet if the pastor does not understand his role and the prophet does not understand his. The two of them must work together as a team. It seems that sometimes the prophet gets the glory because he operates in a certain way and the pastor becomes intimidated. Pastors and prophets will not function properly (singularly or as a team) if they do not know who they are in Christ. Identity is the key to everything! It is not about who gets to shine in the spotlight. It is about dying to "self" so that the Greater One can work through you to get the job done.

The pastor's temperament is different from the prophetic temperament or the prophetic personality. While it is not my intention to review the entire role of pastor, I will say a few differentiating words. The pastor is the shepherd who walks with the sheep and cares for them. He is there for the process of faith. When a prophet sees something in the Spirit, he wants it done *now*, because that is how he sees it being done. Part of being a prophet means grasping the word of God as if it were immediately present. But everything cannot be done "now." Some things must wait. If a pastor is the senior man, then the prophet has to become subject to the pastor.

The relationship between a pastor and a prophet has the potential for conflict. But it is a valuable relationship that helps to balance out the functions of each person. A prophet helps to equip the saints. Some prophets become egotistical, thinking, *I am better than the rest of the leadership because I am a prophet. I am the best God has, so I am going to dominate.* But the words of God are never given through one person only, nor fulfilled in them. The only person to do that is Christ. Instead, we are all given different gifts, different roles, in order that we might see our functioning together as Christ's power. Without this kind of dependence, there would be much danger and temptation if only one person were in leadership over all and claiming to know the words of God.

Prophets are foundation stones, but they are not the chief cornerstone. There is a difference. Jesus is the chief cornerstone who holds all the other stones (apostles and prophets) together. Prophets must never believe that they are the "top dog."

A prophet's ministry must be judged by another prophet or the local leadership. In 1 Corinthians 14, there are guidelines for the Corinthian church as to how to function together:

> If there is no interpreter, the speaker should keep quiet in the church and speak to himself and to God. Two or three prophets should speak, and the others should weigh carefully what is said. And if a revelation comes to someone who is sitting down, the first speaker should stop. For you can all prophesy in turn so that everyone may be instructed and encouraged. The spirits of prophets are subject to the control of prophets. For God is not a God of disorder but of peace—as in all the congregations of the Lord's people.
>
> 1 Corinthians 14:28–33

Some prophets do not like to be judged by other prophets. They say, "I hear from God. I can judge myself." This attitude is wrong! The Bible says that prophecy must be judged. It says to despise not prophesying and prove all things. How are you going to prove prophecy if you do not judge it? Hold fast to those things that are good (see 1 Thessalonians 5:20–21), which means that some things that some prophets say might not be good because the prophet is still an imperfect vessel. Prophecy must be judged.

A lot of people say, "The prophetic word you gave me does not confirm with me." In other words, it is not what they are "used" to doing. There is a comfort zone set up in everyone's life that we construct out of the fabric of our life structure. We are not even aware that we do it, but we are human, and that means we love to find the comfortable place where everything in our lives fits into the mode we built. In dealing with a personal prophetic word, we need to remember that God tells us things that break us out of our comfort zones. God hopes to tear down the walls that isolate us from others in order to make us more transparent vessels. On this side of heaven, we will never be perfected, which means that we are meant to keep growing and changing. The mediocrity that each person has set up in their lives must be challenged by the voice of the Lord in order to bring about a change and a shifting from one level of glory to another.

If you received a word and it has not been confirmed yet, wait until it is confirmed. The Bible says if two or three witnesses shall agree, every word will be established. Another word for *established* is *confirmed*.

Prophets today no longer move in the mode that we know as *inscripturation*. The Old Testament prophets moved in this mode. Inscripturation is new revelation that becomes authoritative as Scripture. This is obviously the highest level of prophetic revelation (see 2 Timothy 3:16). God breathed it (*theopneustos* in Greek) on them, so it was not judged. Such revelation is not given anymore. In the New Testament age, prophets are not in the same order as the Old Testament prophets. God tells us to judge prophecy in the New Covenant.

> For we know in part, and we prophesy in part. But when that which is perfect is come, then that which is in part shall be done away. When I was a child, I spake as a child, I understood as a child, I thought as a child: but when I became a man, I put away childish things. For now we see through a glass, darkly; but then face to face: now I know in part; but then shall I know even as also I am known.
>
> 1 Corinthians 13:9–12, KJV

New Testament prophets know in part and prophesy in part and see through a glass darkly. God has given them only a part; that is why it has to be judged. If God has given you a part here and a part there, you must gather those pieces together, as if you are building a bridge. Each piece put together and joined to the whole will help you cross that bridge, but if you keep them in pieces or misplace or ignore some of them, you are going to end up in the river.

Prophets receive information in different ways. Abraham encountered God in a deep sleep (see Genesis 15:12). Ezekiel was lifted up in the Spirit (see Ezekiel 3:14; 8:3). Daniel dreamed and Peter received in a trance. Different words come to people differently.

But if you have been called to the office of the prophet, it means you can prophesy at will in the same way a pastor or teacher operates at will. Embrace your fit and celebrate Jesus the Prophet inside of you.

And one other thing . . . it is okay to feed the prophet's belly! A lot of confusion has surrounded feeding the belly of the prophet. You cannot just walk into a doctor's office or a psychiatrist's practice, lay there and let them diagnose you, and then simply get up and walk out. You have got to pay those so gifted and learned. When you pay them, what you are actually doing is feeding them. The office of the prophet is a profession, and unless you feed their bellies, they cannot eat! It is a slap in the face of a prophet if you come to them and ask them for a prophetic word and not feed them. That is an insult not only to that prophet but also to God, who has promised to provide for them.

"And Elijah said unto her, Fear not; go and do as thou hast said: but make me thereof a little cake first, and bring it unto me, and after make for thee and for thy son" (1 Kings 17:13, KJV). Notice when the miracle took place for this woman: after she fed the belly of the prophet. She was instructed to feed his belly first. After feeding his belly, the miracle came. The office of the prophet entails more than just prophesying; it is actually a profession, just as being a lawyer, doctor or teacher is someone's profession. This is this man's livelihood; this is what he does for a living.

"Amos answered Amaziah, 'I was neither a prophet nor the son of a prophet, but I was a shepherd, and I also took care of sycamore-fig trees'"(Amos 7:14). The prophet Amos was saying, "My mother and my father were not prophets, but yet the Lord called me into the office of a prophet." The office of the prophet was a generational gift, handed down from one generation to another.

That is why lineages were so important in Scripture: Whoever made up your lineage determined who you were. If there were no prophets in your lineage, then you had no business prophesying, being a prophet or holding that office. That is why Amos was so overwhelmed when God called him to the prophetic office. He said, "*Neither* my mother nor my father were prophets—how can You be calling me to be a prophet, Lord?" God simply interrupted the generational cycle for His particular purpose. In His sovereignty, He can do what He wants to do. Even so, it is basically generational. I am a prophet because someone or a group of people in my lineage were prophets.

A prophet must have a commission. You have to have a call. God has to give you something to prophesy about. There must be a word in your mouth—not simply a bunch of rambling words, but a specific word. When God spoke to Moses, He put a specific word in Moses' mouth. He told Moses to "go down and tell Pharaoh to let My people go." That was the word of the Lord placed in Moses' mouth. The specific word comes with the commission. If there is no specificity in your word, then you should not prophesy or claim to be a prophet.

Prophets Must Be Tough, Yet Gentle

A prophet must be a criticizer of the social establishments. In some cases, he pushes, providing the necessary thrust to individuals and nations to compel them into God's purpose. Other times, he pulls, furnishing the energy required to yank the reluctant into God's purpose. Either way, he is usually an unwanted, unheralded defender of truth.

Very often in the Old Testament, prophets were not happily received. The words they offered were not always what people wanted to hear, because God is merciful, but He is also just. He often used His prophets to speak justice and correction to His people. When they were wayward, He would send a prophet to speak to them. Hosea is a good example of this. God told him to marry a prostitute and have children with her. In this, God was drawing an allegory for His own loving commitment to Israel. Yet God's judgment was present as well, as He allowed suffering to happen to Hosea's children and the Hebrew people. In the same way that a father loves his children and corrects them, the Lord of the Old Testament was pursuing His people, longing for their best interests.

In the New Testament, Jesus set the example for prophets and prophecy. He showed grace and mercy to the lowliest of people yet exercised severe judgment on those who deserved it. He was a criticizer of the social establishment of His day. Sadducees, Pharisees and scribes composed the social order of that time. When Jesus confronted them, He called them vipers, snakes and dogs (see Matthew 7:6; 12:34; 23:33). He called them animals because of the way they treated other people, particularly the poor. It was not that Jesus did not love them or that He cut them off as people; it was that the Sadducees and Pharisees were not carrying out God's plans for His people. They were wayward, and He was delivering the message of God to them—the prophetic word.

In the same way, a modern-day prophet is able to hold both judgment and mercy, justice and grace. As a prophet, he must serve to energize his people. Jesus demonstrated two natures, or characters: a lion and a lamb. To those who oppressed the poor, He was seen as a lion of prey. He went out and devoured those who sought to keep down and oppress the poor. To a person under oppression, Jesus was viewed as a lamb—gentle, meek and kind.

Isaiah was able to say, "Comfort, comfort my people, says your God. Speak tenderly to Jerusalem, and proclaim to her that her hard service has been completed, that her sin has been paid for, that she has received from the LORD's hand double for all her sins" (Isaiah 40:1–2). Yet Isaiah was also to give the word,

> The LORD is angry with all nations; his wrath is on all their armies.
> He will totally destroy them, he will give them over to slaughter.
> Their slain will be thrown out, their dead bodies will stink; the
> mountains will be soaked with their blood.
>
> Isaiah 34:2–3

The dual nature that Isaiah and Jesus demonstrated is the same that a prophet has to demonstrate. In an appropriate sense, a prophet has to be dualistic. He must demonstrate the nature of a lion and devour those who are oppressing God's people. At the same time, a prophet has to demonstrate the character of a lamb and show kindness, meekness and humility. He must seek to aid the oppressed and those who are bound by poverty. Dualism in this case means inhabiting both the transcendent "other-mindedness" of God and the immanent "present time and space" incarnate action of Jesus as God.

Along these lines, the name Jesus is literally translated as "liberator." By being a representative of Christ, a prophet must engage in the struggle for freedom. If you are not willing to get involved, then you are not willing to become a prophet. In almost every biblical situation, a prophet was called to "go" to a person or a people group to share the word of the Lord. You have to roll up your sleeves and get involved in the fight. God did not tell Jonah to write a letter to Nineveh; He told him to go. It is not easy, for it is a struggle. Nonetheless, it is a fight in which we must become involved if we wish to align our lives with God's heart. A prophet must stand and be counted. And not in just any willy-nilly fight. This is not about getting all riled up over what this verse means or what that old hymn is really trying to say! No, entering the prophetic nature of Jesus Christ—the Liberator—means being sent to the poor, the helpless and the hopeless, the people in great darkness who would see a great light. This is the role of the prophet.

The mantle of the prophetic office is demanding. It puts us in some very unusual positions and situations. Most of us do not like being confrontational. A prophet, however, must be confrontational. Moses was asked to tell Pharaoh to let the Israelites go. How do you think this would go over, an exiled, fallen prince asking Pharaoh to give up his empire? Isaiah was told to tell King Hezekiah he would, indeed, die. Would it be easy to deliver a death sentence to a king (see Isaiah 38:1)? Since God has called the prophet, there is a good chance it is to deliver His judgment word. It is important for him to be confrontational because he is God's spokesman, expressing God's feelings and attitude in a particular situation. Thus the prophet has to get involved in the fight. He has to open his mouth and blow the trumpet!

The prophet must make some issues plain. He has to speak out against injustice, which is, in essence, confrontation. You develop a lot of enemies when you do this. Very few people will side with you because you are speaking out against issues and situations that uncover those who seek to oppress.

The prophet must speak of God-given alternatives for His people. As he gets into the struggle for freedom, he will begin to express to them an alternative to their oppression. We may feel at times that our circumstances and situations are unceasing, as if we are continually going in circles. A prophet will break certain cycles that hang over your life. He brings freedom for you in the areas of finances and health, and freedom from chains that have you bound hand and foot. He will give you an alternative to what exists in your society. You may be confronted with racism, but God will give you an alternative plan of freedom.

Prophets Nurture and Protect the Flock

In order for a prophet to most effectively minister, she has to understand people's cultural backgrounds and traditions. She must know what makes them tick. She has to know where, how and why they hurt. She has to be sensitive to their needs. The Bible says that Jesus was touched by the feelings of our infirmities (see Matthew 20:34; 14:14). He understood us. He became one of us so that He could understand where we are coming from. He understood our backgrounds, cultures and traditions. He knew what we suffered and He knew the pain that we had to bear. In order for me to bring a change in your life, I have to know what you are going through. I have to know what you are experiencing. The only way for me to know that is to be identified with your culture and tradition.

The function of the prophetic ministry is to nurture. Nurturing is actually "building up." After a woman has a child, she begins to nurture it. She helps that child grow. The responsibility of the prophet is to nurture people to help them to grow. Once he brings liberation to them, they become like babes who need to be nurtured. In an Old Testament metaphor, God would devastate His people and take away all they held dear in order that He might bring them into the desert, where He could comfort them, speak tenderly to them and win their hearts back. Nurturing is another aspect of the prophetic ministry in which the prophets instill in the hearts of God's people God's directive for their growth. He directs them in the areas of increase and expansion.

The prophetic ministry evokes consciousness. Prophets have to make you aware of the things of which you are unaware. Jesus restored sight to the blind. There are many people who can see physically, yet are blind. Scripture tells us that the god of this age has blinded their hearts to the light of Christ (see 2 Corinthians 4:4). When certain misconceptions and misunderstandings are first laid before us, we believe them to be the truth until a greater truth is laid next to them. A prophet opens your eyes to falsehoods by providing a greater truth.

The Bible says that Jesus opened the eyes of the blind, giving them sight and making them aware. He gave them a sense of consciousness to make them aware of the things that were actually taking place around them. When they looked at the prevailing conditions, they felt hopeless. They felt that there was no way out and no means of survival. But Jesus showed them the truth. He brought them a sense of consciousness and awareness that they did not have before.

Prophets Reform the Social Order

A prophet must be a reformist. The word *reform* means "to change." Change is a prophetic move of God. As a reformist, a prophet is in a position of having to take a situation and turn it around with his words. It is not an easy task. This is the mantle of Isaiah, Jeremiah and Ezekiel, men whose God-given words shaped new worlds. It is difficult to take something that already exists, stop it, reverse it and change it to work for the benefit of others. There are things that presently exist that have to be changed. There are groups of people who are not benefiting from existing structures—these structures must be torn down. They must be reestablished and reconstructed, reformed and changed into another image.

God has a tendency to raise up prophets in order to bring reformation and change to His people. If something is not benefiting everyone, it has to change. If it only benefits a minority—like the elite, the powerful, the wealthy or the ruling race—it has to change. God is concerned about the oppressed: the weak, the poor, the widow, the fatherless, the illegal alien and the ethnic minority.

God acts through His prophets to achieve His purpose against oppression—against His enemy. Whenever you see a prophet prophesying against oppression, understand that he is conveying God's attitude, mood or feeling concerning that issue. God communicates His heart and mind to the prophet. In turn, the prophet conveys the heart and mind of God to the people. When God is dealing with oppression, He usually speaks in terms of injustice. God does not tolerate injustices anywhere, and He does not care who is exercising the unjust actions. It is as though God is saying, through the prophet, that He will not stand by and be diminished through the actions of the oppressor. He will overturn tables, empires and the hearts of men and women in order to make things right.

He does not tolerate injustice coming from anyone. Whether it might be race against race or individual against individual, God does not tolerate it. He is a God of judgment; yet He is a God of love and peace. This can be simplified into God standing in judgment against hate and violence. God judges that which is less than His perfect love and peace that passes understanding. Prophets are the human vehicles through which God's position in a situation can be realized. They know what God is saying concerning the situations of life, the issues with which we are confronted. As God gives His people a heightened awareness of the things He will not tolerate, you will hear more and more prophets proclaiming God's intolerance.

The prophet must show an interest in God's way of bringing freedom. A prophet cannot have his own ideas or plans to bring liberty to the people of God. He must wait on God to give him a plan of redemption so that he can proclaim it to the people. Moses was given a plan by God to bring liberation to the Israelites. They did not simply get up and walk out. God raised up a leader for them and expressed to that leader His plan to bring freedom to that people. In following them, the leader, Moses, recapitulated the thoughts and the mind of God concerning freedom, bringing the people out of bondage and into liberation.

The prophet declares redemption through prophecy. Redemption is actually a work of freedom, a process of liberation. Jesus redeemed us from sin and freed us from sin. Again, this is what His name literally means—Liberator. Is this not amazing? The Great Emancipator is on our side! He is about the work of liberating hearts and lives!

The prophet must incite the people of God to challenge oppression. The prophet speaks in such a way that it will incite the people not to be satisfied with their present conditions. He will anger them, making them so mad at their condition that they will desire change. He will speak to their hearts so they themselves will become intolerant of injustice.

Further, a prophet needs to understand old prophetic movements in order to comprehend new ones. Things often occur in cycles: Whatever happened before will happen again. After all, there is nothing new under the sun. In fact, we could say that whatever *God* did before, He is going to do again. His patterns and principles are foundational and repetitive. We understand how God is going to move in the latter days or in days to come by simply examining what took place historically in God's Word. One of the ways we understand the plan of liberation is by looking at the story of Moses. The bondage of the Israelites in Egypt is very much the same as our bondage under certain social orders.

A helpful understanding of this comes from considering the symbolism of Egypt in the life of God's people. One of the first times Egypt appears in Scripture is when Abraham journeys there in order to escape famine. While there, he lies in order to protect himself. We begin to see that while Egypt may be a safe place, it is also a place where integrity goes down the drain. Safe, secure and shallow. This is confirmed in the book of Exodus: Egypt, full of grain, full of provision for a time, has now become a place of bondage to the children of Israel. They are enslaved. Have you not seen this before? The very thing that brings fulfillment and security, that even seems like provision, turns into a source of slavery. This can be true financially. Materially. Relationally. Communally. Even spiritually, I have witnessed people turn God's provisions into enslaving factors.

But hallelujah for the liberating power of God; while we are yet enslaved in Egypt, He sends a deliverer. This is the true miracle of Moses. God invades the place of bondage, and from the inside He tears it apart! In fact, this is what God does every day. He is still liberating, still raising up a Moses. He is still freeing His people from the oppression that is so easy to slip into when safety and security are our primary goals. The knowledge of how God did this in the past informs how we prophetically know what He is about today.

The actions of a prophet must be much like that of a madman. His message, his method of delivery and even his image may appear odd to many. Consider John the Baptist. People thought he was crazy. When they observed his demeanor (eating bugs), his style of dress (wearing camel's hair) and where he resided (in the wilderness), they thought he had lost his mind. When he encountered the house of Herod, he began to speak out against Herod's sin. Protocol prohibited anyone from challenging the king's orders or sins. Herod did not like what John had to say, and it did not help John's situation that people thought he was some sort of nut. They threw him in a dungeon because they believed he had lost his mind.

But that is the character of some prophets. Their words may be hard to swallow, and it may seem as though they have lost their minds when they begin confronting certain issues. John the Baptist was simply telling the truth about Herod. When we tell the truth about certain issues, we will be viewed as madmen or enemies. People will try to stifle our voices to suppress the truth. Some even thought Jesus was mad, and they sought to imprison and silence Him, too.

The prophet must disrupt the imperial order. There must be a dismantling. If it does not happen at the foundation, it will happen at the top, and rebellion will result. This is why there is such a push and pull where the prophetic office is concerned. It is just not enough to see one group of people enjoying life in apparent abundance when another group has absolutely nothing.

5

The Prophet As Seer

Elijah versus Elisha; Joel

The prophetic word comes like energy that must flow.
So let it flow.

 *S*ome things are to say, and some things are to pray. Learn the difference between the two. Not every beautiful picture you see in the Spirit is to be "hung on the wall" at this time. Sometimes we need to pray about the things we see about others until God says, "It's time for Me to hang them up."

The Power of the Seer

The ministry of the seer plays a very important role in the establishment of the Church in this day. This term, *seer,* is not used much in Christian churches, nor is it really understood. Even though the Bible refers to seers in the Old Testament, they play a vital role in the New Testament, as well. That role has to do with the office of the prophet established by Christ according to Ephesians 4. All seers are prophets, but not all prophets are seers. Because I do a lot of traveling when I preach and prophesy, I minister with different kinds of prophets. I consider myself a *nabi* prophet, one who has a "bubbling up" of prophetic *words* in his spirit (*nabi* in Hebrew means to "bubble up" or "gush out"). The seer is one who sees in *picture* or *vision* form.

A *nabi* prophet can, within a second, sense the bubbling up of a prophetic word in his spirit and speak it forth. This is different from the seer, who must wait for it, see it and then speak it. Both ministries are vitally important in the Church today. These ministries can balance each other in the prophetic realm.

What Is the Seer Ministry?

A seer sees the unseen and hears the unspoken cries. His heart is attuned to the voice of the Father and of Christ—he does what he sees the Father doing and speaks what he hears the Father speaking. The concept comes from two Hebrew words, *hozeh* and *ro'eh,* which simply translate as "someone who sees." They are used in the books of Amos and Ezekiel (see Amos 7:12; Ezekiel 13:9).

First Samuel 9:8–10 tells the story of Saul and his servant consulting a seer:

> The servant answered him again. "Look," he said, "I have a quarter of a shekel of silver. I will give it to the man of God so that he will tell us what way to take." (Formerly in Israel, if someone went to inquire of God, they would say, "Come, let us go to the seer," because the prophet of today used to be called a seer.) "Good," Saul said to his servant. "Come, let's go." So they set out for the town where the man of God was.

What Is the Seer For?

In the New Testament we read about the fivefold ministry of Christ: the apostle, the prophet, the evangelist, the pastor and the teacher

(Ephesians 4:11–13). These ministries were given for what purpose? So that the body would mature to the point when the fivefold ministry of Christ would no longer be necessary. When everyone would know the Lord from the least to the greatest. The seer ministry is what I like to call the "eye of God." They see only what the Lord sees and hear only what the Lord says.

The seer Joel saw a vision from the Lord for the people of Judah. In Joel 1, he had told the people that the plagues and droughts they were suffering had come from the Lord. In his vision, he described what would happen to them:

> Blow a trumpet in Zion, and sound an alarm on My holy mountain! Let all the inhabitants of the land tremble, for the day of the LORD is coming; surely it is near, a day of darkness and gloom, a day of clouds and thick darkness. As the dawn is spread over the mountains, so there is a great and mighty people; there has never been anything like it, nor will there be again after it to the years of many generations.
>
> A fire consumes before them and behind them a flame burns. The land is like the garden of Eden before them but a desolate wilderness behind them, and nothing at all escapes them. Their appearance is like the appearance of horses; and like war horses, so they run. With a noise as of chariots they leap on the tops of the mountains, like the crackling of a flame of fire consuming the stubble, like a mighty people arranged for battle.
>
> Before them the people are in anguish; all faces turn pale. They run like mighty men, they climb the wall like soldiers; and they each march in line, nor do they deviate from their paths. They do not crowd each other, they march everyone in his path; when they burst through the defenses, they do not break ranks.
>
> They rush on the city, they run on the wall; they climb into the houses, they enter through the windows like a thief. Before them the earth quakes, the heavens tremble, the sun and the moon grow dark and the stars lose their brightness. The LORD utters His voice before His army; surely His camp is very great, for strong is he who carries out His word. The day of the LORD is indeed great and very awesome, and who can endure it?

Joel 2:1–11, NASB

Can you see the difference between a *nabi* prophet and a seer? One small distinguishing factor is that a prophet's words can be more direct—"this will happen" or "that will happen." A seer's words can take on a sometimes poetic quality—"all faces turn pale," "the moon grows dark and the stars lose their brightness." A prophet can speak of action and outcome. A seer may speak of tone and mood.

Both the seer and the *nabi* prophet are called to be prayer warriors and sometimes watchmen on the wall. A seer prophet sometimes will see but is not allowed to say; in other words, some things are to say and some things are to pray. This is an inward journey.

Very often a seer is known by another term in Christian circles: *prayer warrior* or *intercessor*. These are not synonymous with *seer,* but often those who have the personality and the heart to pray for long periods of time or to pray with a single-minded focus are the same ones to whom God has given the ability to "see" into the heart of God. If a seer is told not to speak something but only to pray it, this can often take the form of intercession.

Some examples of seers in the Old Testament are Samuel, Elijah, Elisha, Jeremiah and Ezekiel. Each of them was directed to speak a word that brought down kingdoms and changed the age. God is speaking words to His prophets today that execute His will in the earthly realm.

There are many ways that God speaks to seers; dreams and visions are but one of them. Until seers come to the place of open visions, which will happen, power given to them by the Holy Spirit enables them to understand what is transpiring in the realm just beyond our sight. People think of heaven as a distant realm when in actuality it is only a different level of the reality in which we live. As Christ spoke, "In My Father's house are many dwelling places"; it is His desire that they also be where He is (John 14:2–3, NASB). That is what I would call "taking the high call of Christ Jesus." Until we reach that place of communion with the Lord, we are on a journey that is taking us higher and higher—to a higher and deeper consciousness of our oneness with Christ, the Father and the Holy Spirit (see John 17). The role of the seer and the *nabi* in the Church today is to bring us to that realm of heaven in our everyday lives.

As we ascend more and more into the depths of the presence of God we become acutely aware of everything within the realm of God's Kingdom—for God is spirit, and we are being called to walk and live in this realm. Our awareness cannot become "selective," as if we can choose what we will accept or reject. We become aware of God's entire Kingdom, which includes many things we do not even have in our vocabulary yet. We must be careful to stay open to all that He will bring to us, not to have any preconceived ideas, but just to stay open and let Him teach us. The role of the seer and *nabi* is to bring revelation about what has been, what is and what is to come. There are things that will be revealed to us through the prophetic ministry that will ultimately change our mindsets and possibly our theology. We must allow this wonderful ministry of the prophetic to show us things we like and things we do not like. This is the job of the prophetic: to display all the things that God in His Kingdom reign wants us to know and have.

What I am trying to do with this word is create an awareness of something that is available. One of the greatest keys to change is simply realizing that it is available. There is such a deadness on this age, a dullness, an absolute unawareness of anything spiritual aside from what is termed "psychic" or "spiritual." Coming to the realization that the provisions of God are available now changes the dynamics of everything.

Every provision for sonship, for resurrection life and for the *zoe* (life) of God are here now, locked up inside the mouth of the prophetic realm. We must begin to open the door of the prophetic and let the King (and His provision and truth) come in so He can ultimately reign.

In Los Angeles in the early 1900s, a revival took place that is credited with starting the Pentecostal movement in America. The Azusa Street revival grew on the earnestness of the people's prayers. They spent days and weeks together in prayer, asking for a full baptism of the Holy Spirit. People tarried before the Lord because they realized that there was something more of God available than they had yet experienced. They had heard rumors of baptisms in the Spirit that were starting to happen throughout Europe, but nothing had really come over to America yet. But there were these believers, waiting before the Lord, looking for the experience of this new thing that God was doing. And when it began, they realized that something was available to them that they had not seen before. As they began to wait on the Lord, believer after believer began to be baptized in the Spirit, speaking in tongues and being empowered by the Holy Spirit. Others to whom this experience was still rather vague were not entering into it. It was not until something clicked and they believed, realizing that it was available, that the experience began to come. Gradually this expanded as thousands grabbed ahold of it.

I draw a comparison because in this hour we are looking for something that has been released, but we have not quite seen it yet. Because of that we have not reached in and taken it. But it is here, and it has been for some time now. When the prophetic is launched out to its full potential and power, we will start to see the nations change and the Kingdom of God come to planet earth. The seer ministry needs to be released to the fullest in order for us to see and behold the wonderful works of God, just like they did on the Day of Pentecost in the book of Acts.

There was a time when the Church labeled all of this demonic and absolutely rejected it. It took many decades before the Church began to accept the baptism of the Spirit as something from God. We face a similar reproach in this hour for the seer ministry.

In the book of Joel it speaks of the Spirit falling on both the believer and the unbeliever alike. God is opening the portals of the Kingdom in this age, and there are many who are tuning in to the realities of this Kingdom age.

> It will come about after this that I will pour out My Spirit on all mankind; and your sons and daughters will prophesy, your old men will dream dreams, your young men will see visions. Even on the male and female servants I will pour out My Spirit in those days.
>
> Joel 2:28–29, NASB

We must realize that God has something greater for His children than we have understood. Whether it is in the realm of dreams or visions, the appearances of Christ or what we have known as out-of-body experiences, it is all within the realm of what God is releasing at this time. I do not want to dwell on out-of-body experiences, but I will say that when I speak of them, I am not speaking of astral projection, a fairly common operation of the soul. I am talking about the power of God moving on a person. We must understand that there are signs and wonders of God that have been given to each one of us. Omnipresence and omniscience are aspects of the Godhead, and they are also aspects of our reality as we move deeper into the realm of sonship.

The subject of dreams and visions has been exhausted. Many books have been written about this topic, and most, if not all of them, address it from the plane of the human soul and the interpretation of vague symbols and signs that one may receive. Understand that this is not what I am talking about. I am talking about walking in an awareness of the realm of Spirit.

How Does God Speak?

If we want to understand when the Lord is speaking to us, we had better learn His language! My friend Dwayne McLean describes four main ways that God speaks to us:

1. Mind pictures. Sometimes a person's face will come to your mind. Whatever that person represents to you could be what the Spirit wants to release into the person to whom you are prophesying.
2. Emotional stirrings. Oftentimes before some event, a service, a prayer meeting, you may feel an emotional stirring. You have a joy or burden that is unrelated to your personal circumstances. If it does not make much sense to your situation, then perhaps He is letting you feel something for someone else. Perhaps you are to use that feeling to release a word for

someone else. Do not be afraid to ask, "Is anyone feeling sad right now? Can I pray for you?"

3. Symbiotic pains. This is physical pain you feel in your body, in empathetic resonance with someone else's pain. Often, if you have been given the gift of healing, you may receive a word of knowledge in the form of feeling the pain of someone else. If your shoulder is twinging, perhaps God intends to heal someone else's shoulder. Ask Him for it. Why not? Speak up. The Spirit has called you to be His voice.

4. Physical sensations. These can take the form of electricity, a tingle, an energy—the numinous! It is the presence of God. You may feel the "fire" of the Spirit in your hands or feet. You may feel a wind even when no air vent is near.

None of these things are explained in Scripture. Neither Jesus nor the apostles spelled out how to heal or what to look for. The Bible is not a manual; it is a historical record. These "methods" can sound hokey. But it gives me peace knowing that people experience the presence of the Spirit in these same ways even when they have not been taught about it. These experiences do not have to be taught; they are experienced. The Spirit of God does not have to be learned. It has to be experienced.

Most people have one or two of these gifts, if not all. The first type of communication, mind pictures, includes dreams and visions. Dreams and visions are a very important aspect of the functioning of the seer ministry. They are a stepping stone into the perfect, into the open vision that is coming. As the seer's body continues to come alive to the spirit realm, that person begins to experience what we have called signs within the body. One of those signs is the enlightenment of the eyes, as the seer begins to actually see into the spirit realm with his or her physical eyes. If you are called to be a seer, you may at first begin to see glimpses. They may be shadows or faint outlines of God's light on His people. The more you practice and record and monitor what you receive in the Spirit, the more it will grow in you. If you respect and honor what the Lord is showing you and you are diligent to listen and to practice,

He will release greater levels of revelation to you. As you continue going through the deep work of the cross, you will gradually move to higher and higher levels in your gift, and your eyes will behold that which you have not seen.

The Lord will sometimes give seers a picture of how all things are to be for creation—the planes of existence that God has birthed for us. It is time for us to enter into that joy and live the *zoe* kind of life that the Lord has prepared for each of us. Dreams and visions in this day are an avenue by which God allows His seers to see and hear as they bring the dead bones of the Church to life again. The more you seek His face, the more you will understand that the visions and dreams that God is giving you are purely an avenue of communication from the Lord to you. The deeper dimensions of dreams and visions are not a function of what you are going through in your soul; they are a way of hearing and seeing what the Spirit offers for your glorious future, the good plans He has toward you.

As it was for Daniel and other prophets of the Old Testament, the visions that come to our minds need interpretation by revelation. We are not doing a mental exercise of dream interpretation; we are seeking the Lord for revelation of the full import of what He is showing. Whether through a dream or vision, allow God to give you the revelation of what is being presented. And we must act on what we receive when a *nabi* or a seer approaches us with a word. This is a small but vital key—act on what you see. When you do this, revelation will eventually come. This is acting on faith.

Seers' Relationships with the Lord

The seer must have a strong relationship with the Lord. Everything we experience, everything we see is about a relationship with the Lord. If you are called to be a seer, this is what it is all about. What visions and dreams you receive and interpret are revealed to you only because there is a dialogue opening up between you and Him. There will come a point at which this transaction is more complete, and what seems as "dreams" will indeed manifest to you more clearly so that you will understand what you are experiencing.

One easy key to begin moving in the seer ministry, and in the realm of dreams and visions, is to simplify your life. In the days of the Old Testament, the shepherds stood guard over their flock. Life was relatively simple. What we face in our electronic age is excessive overstimulation. As great a blessing as the computer is, it is also a curse. This information age is making people more and more cerebral as we constantly deal with input and more input. We are evolving further away from the inherent sensitivity that we have as part of God's creation. We have become like a computer, overly rational, focused on information processing and otherwise very imperceptive.

It is time we start slowing down and take a look at our lives. Television, the foods we eat, the issues that are eating us, the things that bind us and the demands others make on us, the constant stress we live with day in and day out—all affect our sensitivity and alertness to the Spirit. Waiting on God, or meditation, whichever you call it, is pivotal to a deep walk in the Spirit. Simplifying your life on every level is imperative if you have decided to walk in those things God has prepared for you.

We could talk all day about the office of the seer, but understand that the realm of darkness has resisted and fought against the establishment of the seer anointing in the earth—without success. What God is establishing will be done; God's word will not return to Him void! The more time we spend in intimacy with our Lord, the more He can unveil things to the eyes of our hearts through sign and symbol, enabling us to discern between our surface thoughts and what is being directed at us in the Spirit. The Lord has declared, "That which is done in secret shall be made known." This is happening. That which is being done behind closed doors, in secret, in high places, is being made known.

The seer's ministry actually represents a company—perhaps one of the companies spoken of in the book of Revelation (the two witnesses). A company of seers that moves through this age and binds its kings with chains and its nobles with fetters of iron.

This is not a platitude, this is reality. How honored are we that what has been seen only in Scripture is being made manifest in the flesh once again!

One of the greatest assaults the Body of Christ has seen over the past thirty years has been the assault against the birthing or establishment of the seer ministry. In Revelation we are told that the dragon will try to destroy the man-child as he approaches birth. Once again these are just words. What do these words really mean? Who is this man-child who comes to birth in this hour? We know that this man-child represents the sons of God—to whom the prophets speak, decreeing that they should come forth in this hour.

6

Giving Birth to Your Prophetic Word

Ezekiel

Make sure your belly is pregnant with the word of the Lord. That way, in your spiritual nine months, God's dream will become a reality for you.

"I Received a Prophetic Word; Now What?"

Most people rejoice when they receive a prophecy, often expecting the manifestation of it to occur overnight. Nine times out of ten, it will not.

Prophecy is like a baby. Nine months is a typical gestation period, but sometimes babies are born early. A premature baby often has to struggle until her body matures enough to handle being outside of the womb's provision and protection. If questioned, most women emphatically say they do not want to bear a premature child, despite the pain and discomfort they endure carrying a child to term. Why?

Because they understand the risks to themselves and the child, and they realize that having a healthy child who is ready to breathe the air of the world is more important than avoiding pain. They would rather endure the pain for the gain.

The prophetic word is a seed of life. When the word comes to you, it has the same creative power that established the universe. The Bible says, "By the word of the LORD the heavens were made" (Psalm 33:6). If God gifts your spirit with a prophetic word, He is sharing with you that same creative breath.

If you have a prophetic call and gifting and then you come together with other prophets, you receive fresh energy and the word springs up within you. Suddenly your flow is mightier and stronger because you have come into the company of prophets. Saul, for example, began to prophesy when he came into the company of prophets (see 1 Samuel 10:10–11).

A prophetic word has a timetable: It has an appointed time, a particular season when it is going to come to pass. A seed planted in the earth passes through a specific period of growth before it is ready to bring forth a harvest. Likewise, your prophecy has a period of time during which it will mature and produce a harvest.

When the prophetic word comes to you, it is already preprogrammed for success, preprogrammed to accomplish the things God intends for it to accomplish. We are the only ones who can abort it. No devil can abort your word; only you can choose to do that. Unplanned pregnancies sometimes cause parents to consider aborting their child; but when God delivers a word to you through a prophet, it is not unplanned. He has already planned for you to hear the word, even if you feel surprised by it. If you are pregnant with the word of the Lord, do not be troubled as you wait with expectation. It will come to pass. "For the vision is yet for an appointed time, but at the end it shall speak, and not lie: though it tarry, wait for it; because it will surely come, it will not tarry" (Habakkuk 2:3, KJV).

Every prophetic word you receive is for an appointed day and time. It is the same as if you schedule a doctor's appointment one month in advance; you plan for it by scheduling it into your day. But you do not spend thirty days worrying about whether the doctor will be in. You just show up for the appointment, knowing you are expected on that day. This may seem confusing because waiting on the Lord for the fulfillment of prophecy may take a length of time that we cannot predict. The believers of the Azusa Street revival did not know when the baptism of the Spirit would fall on them, but they kept praying. When a word is received, the word itself carries the promise of fulfillment at a certain time. Even if God has not given you a date or a time frame, expect your prophecy to come to pass because God will come with the manifestation in hand.

Birthing the Prophetic

Giving birth to prophecy is as intricate a process as giving birth to a child.

God says, "So shall my word be that goeth forth out of my mouth: it shall not return unto me void, but it shall accomplish that which I please, and it shall prosper in the thing whereto I sent it" (Isaiah 55:11, KJV). The word of the Lord is powerful. It contains the same life-giving potential as does a seed. And just like the life cycle of a seed—which matures into a plant, flowers, spreads more seeds and eventually dies—the prophetic word also moves in cycles. It speaks death to one season and brings forth life to another. When the prophetic word comes, it may interrupt the cycle you are in. The most common way a woman's menstrual cycle is broken is when a seed is sown and conception takes place. Seeds break cycles.

That is why it is good to come into the presence of godly prophets, because their ministry and words are a visitation from God. New life is conceived as the word is spoken, entering through your being and sinking into the womb of your spirit. Do not miss your day of conception. The day of conception occurs when the word is spoken to your spirit, whether in prayer, in reading, from a prophet or prophetess or from someone sharing prophetically with you. The day of conception is the beginning of the miracle that God is going to bring about. It is the beginning of the idea to which you are going to give birth.

Impregnation in the physical realm begins when the husband and wife come together. When the sperm fertilizes the egg, there is conception. The fertilized egg carries the code for what the child is going to become. It contains everything; the future of the child is already in the seed. Your future is already in the word of prophecy. It is up to you to allow it to incubate and develop inside of you in order for it to come to pass.

Impregnation brings change. When our spirits come together with God's Spirit, impregnation occurs. You are a pregnant man or a pregnant woman. When impregnation occurs, a new being comes to life within a woman's womb. The vision of God—the plan and purpose of God—is now inside of you. It is a child that you are carrying in the womb of your spirit. Inside the vision, like inside the egg, is the set of instructions that when expressed will produce the life of God.

Manifestation of the vision—giving birth—is hard work. Sometimes in her discomfort an expectant mother might say, "I don't like this process," but she perseveres through it. Sometimes there are emotional highs and lows. But the mother hangs in there because she is awaiting a joy-filled birth. In order to give birth to your prophecy, you have to labor with it, just as a pregnant woman must undergo labor pains to bring forth her child. You might say, "God, I don't want to do this!" But when the prophetic word comes, it changes your life, because the word is a new life.

The Divine Catch-Up

The prophetic word brings forth divine order. When our lives are not moving in step with God's program, He sends a prophetic word to realign and reactivate us. It brings correction. When a prophetic word comes to you, it speaks death to one season and the beginning of a new season. It has both a death certificate and a birth certificate attached to it. In the natural realm, the season you are in might feel prolonged, but in the realm of the Spirit, the season has ended.

The Hebrew word for prophecy is *dabar,* which means "to drive forward that which is behind." So if your life is lacking, the prophetic word drives forward what is behind. Many times a prophetic word addresses the potential of what God has made you to be, while what you are experiencing might be totally different.

A prophetic word does not, 100 percent of the time, confirm the revelation that you already have. Some say that the word of the Lord must always be for confirmation. I differ with them.

When God spoke to the widow to sustain Elijah, she did not know sustenance was even possible. God told Elijah the arrangement He had made: "I have commanded a widow there to feed you" (1 Kings 17:9, ESV). The prophetic word does not always confirm what is in your heart; it might speak to some things you have not even conceptualized. It does not always speak to your current experience. Through His prophet, God may speak that He has gifted you to teach, preach or prophesy, while you have never done it before. The word propels that which is behind to come forward.

The person who receives the prophecy is not the same person who fulfills it. When Joseph was seventeen, God spoke to him through a dream. God gave him a lot of dreams, but he was not the same person when the dreams were fulfilled, because he first had to go through deep difficulties in order for those words to come to pass.

His brothers envied him after he shared his dream with them. You have to know those with whom you can share your dream. If you share your dream with your spiritual half brothers, they might be envious. So you must assess even those God has given you to walk with, because you cannot share your dreams with everyone. You may dream big dreams and want to share them with someone who only knows how to dream small dreams. Compared to you, the person is small-minded. What will happen? The person may become an enemy to your dream and prophetic word.

When Jesus began to walk the earth as the Son of God, working miracles and prophesying, and later returned to His hometown, the

Bible says He could not work mighty works there because of the unbelief of those who were familiar with Him. They knew Him as "the carpenter's son" and could not see Him for who He was. As the Son of God, He was a different man. But they had an I-knew-You-when mindset. They were not able to dream big dreams. They could not see that even though a person might physically look the same, that person might not be the same person on the inside.

If you are not ready for change, then you are not ready for the word of the Lord. If you love what you are doing and testify that "everything is going well, God," then be wary of going into the presence of a prophet; the prophet may see seasons in your life that you do not know about. Your home, business, marriage and church may already have changed, for this happens in the realm of the Spirit first. You will not comprehend what the prophet is saying because your life is not in that place yet. When a prophet peeks into your life and brings the word out, he is telling you some things that are already planned for you.

Turning the Page

Our lives are like a drama. Jesus said, "I'm the alpha and the omega. I'm the beginning and the ending. I'm the Author and the Finisher of your faith." Our stories are already written by Him. At the time that God instructed Joshua and the children of Israel, He was giving them manna. He said, "Prepare you victuals" (Joshua 1:11, KJV). Even though it was the season of manna, He gave them another vision. In the mind and heart of God, the season of manna was ending and a new vision was beginning.

If you have received many, many words, prophet messengers are speaking various seasons into your life, various chapters and pages of your story. A prophet might see page 116 at the end of your book. But do not run off with your word. Let's say that you hear, "Yea, I am raising you up to be an apostle. For you shall be My mouthpiece, and you shall trumpet My Word. And you shall begin to start works over here and works over there. You shall travel the islands and prophesy for Me and raise up churches." If you lack understanding, you will hear that word and rush out to try to start a work. You will be out of order, because just as a seed is planted in the earth, the prophetic word takes time to mature and bring forth a harvest. You do not plant a seed today and receive a harvest in a couple of minutes—unless you are a mosquito. Only a mosquito operates like that; its lifespan is about 36 hours, so it has to be quick.

No, when a prophetic word comes to you, it does not come to pass immediately unless it is a word of knowledge. A word of knowledge speaks of things past and things present. For example, a prophet might say, "I see you at age four and at age twenty," and go on to describe the things he sees in your life at those ages. That is a word of knowledge.

God gives the prophet part of His knowledge concerning you because He wants to erase some things and do some reordering of your lifestyle. Perhaps during a certain season of your life, something was held back, and consequently you are not really moving with the intensity of God. A prophet, moving in the gift of a word of knowledge, begins to erase that thing out of your life so you can be propelled to the next season.

A friend of mine received a word of knowledge when someone prophesied that she wore certain labels. The prophet placed her hands on my friend's collarbone and forehead and said, "Here. Right here you wear labels that are untrue and negative. They say you are not lovely. You are not enough. God wants to remove these labels and give you a new name. Your true name." This event was years ago, and yet my friend still recalls it as a pivotal moment in her self-identification. A time when a part of her was "erased" or corrected for the better—for God to find joy in.

God has purposes for your birth. A child might be born illegitimate; some might think it is a mistake. But in the rare-art world, oftentimes flaws make a piece highly valued for its character—its uniqueness. You might think that your life is a mistake, but it is not. God spoke to Jeremiah, "Before I formed thee in the belly I knew thee; and before thou camest forth out of the womb I sanctified thee, and I ordained thee a prophet unto the nations" (Jeremiah 1:5, KJV). Regardless of your background, God wants you to know that before He formed you in the womb, He knew you. Regardless of where you are, God is calling the prophets to arise and come forth. He is forming His prophetic network.

Jeremiah had excuses, but God let him know He had set Jeremiah apart. Do you realize that you were a word in the mind of God before you came to be? The Bible says, "The Word became flesh" (John 1:14). Jesus' life was prophesied beforehand, and later He became flesh. Likewise, God had you in mind before you were placed in your mother's womb. You are not an accident. You were preprogrammed by God and sent into the nationality, race and culture of His choosing. You are not a mistake!

So God wants to settle it now. If you were called to be a prophet or a pastor, it is not an accident. Before the foundation of the world, God planned it and executed His plan for you to walk in that calling now. God planned you to be here before the world even existed. The Bible says that "whom [God] did *foreknow,* he also did predestinate to be conformed to the image of his Son" (Romans 8:29, KJV, emphasis mine). He put you into a set part and a set plan. You were destined before you began to be formed in your mother's womb.

So get rid of your hang-ups. Get rid of all the clichés and the pity party—because God called you, even before you were born!

Conception's Company

Recall God's word to Jeremiah: "Before I formed thee in the belly I knew thee" (Jeremiah 1:5, KJV). We do not choose the will of God; we *discover* the will of God. *Predestination* means "to be destined before connected." God has already orchestrated your purpose. Ezekiel received his call to find an army in the valley of dry bones. So for you: Begin to call for the new prophetic network. Raise it up, and then, as in the valley of dry bones, the bones will join together, end to end, joint to joint, until there is a full frame. Regardless of who you are or what your nationality, God is calling you to come to the summit. Come to the high point to receive.

When a woman is pregnant, she may lose touch with friends who are not pregnant or not mothers, because there are no new instructions she can receive from them. She now links with those who are either in an advanced stage of pregnancy or who have already borne children. Her frame will grow; she will expand to make room for the new life within. Her clothes will change and so probably will her friends. Nothing is as it was. Likewise, when you are pregnant with a prophetic word, you have to seek out those who are pregnant with the same revelation. If you try to share what you are carrying with someone who does not understand, he or she may even cause you to miscarry. "Can two walk together, except they be agreed?" (Amos 3:3, KJV).

When Mary became pregnant by the Holy Ghost, she sought out Elizabeth. She could not have talked to anyone else. She did not discuss it with just anyone because she was pregnant with a new revelation. God provided, leading her to Elizabeth; deep calls to deep. She apparently even had a problem talking with Joseph. He did not understand her conception or her pregnancy, so the angel had to speak with him in order for him to understand that she was carrying God inside of her.

But her cousin Elizabeth, who was six months' pregnant, had a similar—not exact, but similar—miraculous pregnancy. Her husband doubted when God told him that his wife would become pregnant. So Mary and Elizabeth, in similar situations and with similar words given to them by God, sought each other out and found solace in one another.

The purpose of Elizabeth's son, John the Baptist, was to prepare the way for the Lord to come. Thus were the children of Mary and Elizabeth interlocked. One was a forerunner of the other. God will always give you a forerunner for your ministry; someone will pave the way for you. He will make a way for you to walk easily.

As I mentioned, there will be dangers throughout the birthing process and the gestation process. There will be enemies to your dream. Judas was ordained to accompany Jesus. Every great man and woman of God knows that his or her God-given dream—his or her pregnancy—will have a Judas assigned to it. But it is not for you to be afraid of Judas, and it is not for you to pray Judas away. This person has a divine purpose in your life. He is going to take you to your "Calvary."

Every one of us has a Calvary experience. Your life and the victories you experience are not standing in the death, but in the resurrection, of your vision. When you recognize the Judas in your midst, do not pray him away—and do not call him by name, either. When Jesus' hour came, He did not call Judas by his name. Jesus knew all the time who and what Judas was, even when He chose Judas to follow him. But He said, "*One* of you is going to betray me" (see John 13:21).

You see, you do not have to name Judas because Judas knows who he is. He will do what he has to do. Adversity brings growth. The adversity you are propelled into will grow the child within you.

God gave you the power of decision. Follow the fine points of prophecy. There is always a fine print in prophecy; follow the instructions of the Lord. When a woman is pregnant, she is instructed to change her diet in order to nourish the baby as best she can. She may not like it, but it is for the benefit of both the mother and the baby. The Lord will show you the nutrients needed to nourish your word, the life inside of you.

You were preprogrammed for success. The word given to you was preprogrammed for success, because it is the life of God. If God is speaking something through His prophets or by His Spirit into your spirit, it will be successful because not much can stop it. When you were born again, your spiritual genes were transformed. You were given the genes of your Father. Nothing can stop the dream, nothing can stop the vision and nothing can stop the prophetic word but you.

The word of prophecy will grow from its God-given power. This can be trusted. Yet things can get extremely confusing extremely fast if a word is not entirely trustworthy. In the next chapter, we will cover an essential wisdom in encountering the prophetic: What if the word you receive is incorrect? How will you know?

7

Right Word or Wrong Word?

Jeremiah

The prophetic word always sets you up for victory . . . always.

Oh No! I Think I Received a Wrong Word!

John Wimber, the late founder of the Vineyard movement, was known for saying, "Faith is spelled *R-I-S-K*." When we take steps of faith to hear from God, it is going to feel risky. When we aim for something high, the risk factor increases.

As we know, prophecy is a weighty issue and a controversial topic. But what if every prophet were right every time? There would be no controversy—everyone would believe. Unfortunately, as long as prophecy continues through human vessels, there is margin for error. The biggest obstacle in the giving and receiving of prophetic words is the fact that they come from a perfect God and are spoken through imperfect lips. The human element always exists wherever the prophetic word abides. This is true regardless of the level of revelation in the prophetic word.

As you receive words of prophecy—difficult or exhilarating ones—always remember that prophecy is not a guarantee or a commandment; it is an invitation to the privilege of seeing something the way that the Spirit sees it—to see what He sees. The prophet may at times see incorrectly. Prophets are human, lest we forget. We are not above others, and we make mistakes just like everyone else. As we minister, a perfect God is conveying perfect thoughts to our imperfect minds. God has a way of adjusting us in such a way that we are able to express His thoughts and not ours.

Imperfection is not a sin. Oftentimes people think that a mistake that a prophet makes in some area or another is the result of sin in his life. That is not necessarily so. Prophets are imperfect because we are human. Yet we serve a perfect God who has given us a perfect word out of His perfect mind, out of His perfect mouth, through these imperfect lips.

Isaiah cried:

> "Woe to me! . . . I am ruined! For I am a man of unclean lips, and I live among a people of unclean lips, and my eyes have seen the King, the LORD Almighty." Then one of the seraphim flew to me with a live coal in his hand, which he had taken with tongs from the altar. With it he touched my mouth and said, "See, this has touched your lips; your guilt is taken away and your sin atoned for." Then I heard the voice of the Lord saying, "Whom shall I send? And who will go for us?" And I said, "Here am I. Send me!"
>
> Isaiah 6:5–8

The first chapter of Jeremiah relates the same story:

> "Alas, Sovereign LORD," I said, "I do not know how to speak; I am too young."
>
> But the LORD said to me, "Do not say, 'I am too young.' You must go to everyone I send you to and say whatever I command

you. Do not be afraid of them, for I am with you and will rescue you," declares the LORD.

Then the LORD reached out his hand and touched my mouth and said to me, "I have put my words in your mouth. See, today I appoint you over nations and kingdoms to uproot and tear down, to destroy and overthrow, to build and to plant."

Jeremiah 1:6–10

And Moses said unto the LORD, O my Lord, I am not eloquent, neither heretofore, nor since thou hast spoken unto thy servant: but I am slow of speech, and of a slow tongue. And the LORD said unto him, Who hath made man's mouth? or who maketh the dumb, or deaf, or the seeing, or the blind? have not I the LORD? Now therefore go, and I will be with thy mouth, and teach thee what thou shalt say.

Exodus 4:10–12, KJV

Moses was expressing to God his inability and his imperfection. God made Moses this promise: "Do not worry about your imperfections because I will be with your mouth."

Herein lies a fundamental key concerning prophecy. *Is God doing the speaking?* We know that all prophecy must be judged. There must be some type of determination as to whether the word that has been given to you is indeed from God. This is crucial because Satan can speak to you as well and give you harmful directions for your life. He can misguide you, as we read in 2 Chronicles:

Then there came out a spirit, and stood before the LORD, and said, I will entice him. And the LORD said unto him, Wherewith? And he said, I will go out, and be a lying spirit in the mouth of all his prophets. And the LORD said, Thou shalt entice him, and thou shalt also prevail: go out, and do even so.

2 Chronicles 18:20–21, KJV

Never adhere to the words of a lying prophet. There is a vast difference between false prophets and lying prophets. A false "prophet" is not a prophet at all. A lying prophet is a prophet of God who is not telling you the truth concerning the word of the

Lord. See the difference? A man can be a man of God and a prophet but say things that God is not necessarily saying. He may lie for his own personal gain. Whatever the reason, he is neither giving you the mind of God nor expressing to you what is in God's heart. He is simply expressing his own thoughts for his personal reasons.

In Jeremiah 23, Jeremiah is sick in his heart for the lying that is going on in Israel. He bemoans the lying prophets, the ones who only say what people want them to say. "Thus saith the LORD of hosts, Hearken not unto the words of the prophets that prophesy unto you: they make you vain: they speak a vision of their own heart, and not out of the mouth of the LORD" (Jeremiah 23:16, KJV).

If you enjoy being lied to, God will not hold back lies in the mouth of a prophet. Then, like King Ahab, you can hear exactly what you want to hear, rather than what God wants to tell you. Do not stand before a prophet with preconceived ideas. Allow God to speak into your life. Let Him give you His directions and instructions (for, as it says in Titus 1:2, God does not lie).

> The coming of the lawless one will be in accordance with how Satan works. He will use all sorts of displays of power through signs and wonders that serve the lie, and all the ways that wickedness deceives those who are perishing. They perish because they refused to love the truth and so be saved. For this reason God sends them a powerful delusion so that they will believe the lie and so that all will be condemned who have not believed the truth but have delighted in wickedness.
>
> 2 Thessalonians 2:9–12

All Presumptuous Prophecies Are Dangerous

"But the prophet, which shall presume to speak a word in my name, which I have not commanded him to speak, or that shall speak in the name of other gods, even that prophet shall die" (Deuteronomy 18:20, KJV).

If God has *not* instructed you to speak a word, keep your mouth shut. Remember, you will be held accountable for whatever you speak in the name of God. The end result of presumptuousness, the Bible says, is death. Prophets must speak the word of God and nothing more. They cannot speak preconceived ideas. It must surely be the mind of God—not my mind, not your mind, but the mind of God. It is disastrous when a prophet speaks presumptuously. It has an adverse effect on your life and a damaging, destructive effect on the life of a prophet.

Never speak your own mind, for it could get you into a lot of trouble. This is why we are commanded to "possess the mind of Christ." His mind knows *all* the things we will ever need in this life. Without it, you will end up saying the wrong thing at the wrong time. Let God take over your mind and give you what you should and should not say. This is called being partakers of the divine nature of Christ Jesus.

The prophetic word takes on the character of the one ministering. If you have decreased and allow Jesus to increase in you, He is the one who will do the talking in and through you. On the other hand, if a prophet is an evil or destructive person, or if he is a liar, it will be seen. Whatever his character entails will come out in his prophetic ministry. That is why God does not necessarily choose prophets based on ability or capability; He chooses them based on character. God desires to get you to the place of Paul, who said, "For me to live is Christ." Take on the character of Jesus. Operating out of the character of Jesus can impact your life and the lives of those you prophesy to! Whatever kind of person I am will become the foundation of the prophetic word I give you. If I operate as Jesus, I will always give words of "Spirit and life." This is how the prophetic ministry flowed out of Him when He ministered to people.

Unfulfilled Prophecy?

The Law of Confirmation must be applied in order to receive prophecy. This law has two parts: (1) acceptance, which is your part in receiving the prophetic word, and (2) confirmation, which is the

105

prophet's role in giving you the prophetic word. The prophetic word must be accepted by you and received, but it should also confirm something in your life, something that God may have spoken previously. You accept because the word is confirmed in you.

Often, prophetic words are not fulfilled in people because they suffer from a "lack of knowledge"; in other words, they do not understand the language of prophetic principles. People blame the prophet when the word of the Lord does not come to pass, and they might accuse him of not being a prophet of God. In fact, he was; the person just did not do his part in birthing the prophetic word. Though he believed it for a time, as time passed, he began to disbelieve it. He did not allow it to take root inside of him, and it died for lack of nourishment. Time is what God uses to test your faith. You have to consistently accept and believe that word. The moment you fail to exercise faith to see it come to pass is the moment it is never fulfilled. In other words, you abort your prophecy!

When we are dealing with prophecy that has not been fulfilled, it is helpful to understand that there are differences in prophetic function. Do you believe that because you can prophesy God has called you to the prophetic office? This may not be so. There are three consistent functions within the framework of prophecy. The first is the gift of prophecy, which is given by the Holy Ghost, who gives us the ability to demonstrate a particular degree of prophecy. It is better for all believers to prophesy. But that does not necessarily make you a prophet. It does not mean that you can start your own ministry on the corner prophesying to everyone you see. It simply means that God will use you periodically to give a word every now and then whenever He sees fit.

The second function is the Spirit of Prophecy. In our local assembly, the number of prophets we have is evidence that the Spirit of Prophecy resides there. The Spirit of Prophecy enables you to prophesy and give the corporate body a prophetic word whether or not you are a prophet. Again, this does not necessarily make you a prophet. This is where the confusion lies. A lot of people feel that because they move under the gifting of prophecy or because God may have used them on several occasions to prophesy to a local body, it automatically makes them a prophet. Just because you prophesy does not mean you operate in the third function, which is the office of the prophet, discussed in chapter 3.

Prophecy is a sign to the believer and the unbeliever:

> But if an unbeliever or an inquirer comes in while everyone is prophesying, they are convicted of sin and are brought under judgment by all, as the secrets of their hearts are laid bare. So they will fall down and worship God, exclaiming, "God is really among you!"
>
> 1 Corinthians 14:24–25

Paul is describing an unbeliever being drawn to God through the gift of prophecy in these verses. You also see Jesus using prophetic gifts with unbelievers in John 4. His encounter with the Samaritan woman at the well is a great example of the prophetic gift in operation to an unbeliever. We can minister prophetically to businesses, churches and homes, wherever God may lead. Prophecy is for the edification, exhortation and comfort of the Body of Christ and also for convicting the unbelieving heart, drawing sinners to repentance. And it is for instruction, guidance and direction. It brings the Body of Christ into fullness and maturity.

There has been a lot of confusion concerning the use of prophetic gifts. Many prophets are beginning to go out to the highways and byways, prophesying to unbelievers to lead them into the house of God. Prophets today are "taking the Kingdom of God by force." God has instructed prophets to speak into the lives of His people and to give them direction:

> Brethren, be not children in understanding: howbeit in malice be ye children, but in understanding be men. In the law it is written, With men of other tongues and other lips will I speak unto this people; and yet for all that will they not hear me, saith the Lord. Wherefore tongues are for a sign, not to them that believe, but to them that believe not: but prophesying serveth not for them that believe not, but for them which believe.
>
> 1 Corinthians 14:20–22, KJV

Primarily, our assignment is to the Body of Christ unless God otherwise specifies. And He does specify: There were many specific assignments given to men of God in the Bible concerning prophesying to an unbeliever. Moses, who was instructed to speak to Pharaoh, is a great example. But we have to stay in the confines of what God has commanded us to do. If we operate outside of that, we will not find success. If God says to speak to a particular unbeliever, He has a purpose and a reason for it. But as a continuous ministry and service, we have to prophesy to the Body of Christ first.

The prophetic word must serve a purpose. If the word that you are giving is not serving any purpose in someone's life, then you need to hold that word until it becomes mature. If you are sensing something in your spirit and you want to impart understanding to an individual or some insight concerning the mind or heart of God, but it is not serving any particular purpose, then you should hold it. Is this the time for the word to be made known? Is the setting you are in appropriate for receiving the word? My first word to the man in adultery was not necessarily a "good" venue for speaking, though I knew I was to say it. Do you have a sense of peace or calm with the word? Is it from Him? At this point, consider the word a seed that needs to grow. Hold it until it matures and begins to serve a purpose in the life of the person to whom you are going to prophesy.

It is senseless to prophesy to an individual when it has no purpose. What will he or she do with it? Wait until it makes some sense to you before you impart it, so it can make some sense to the individual you are imparting it to. It may not make complete sense to you, but let it be somewhat logical.

The prophetic word must have the right source. Understand that there are different sources from which to acquire insight into future events. There is only one spiritual realm, and both God and Satan are in it. God has the Holy Spirit and angelic spirits who are familiar with aspects of people's lives. Satan has many agents that are familiar with different aspects of people's lives. Our Source is God; He is the source of all of our prophesying. Anything that is emanating from the soul is coming from the realm of demonism.

Familiar spirits are imparting understanding to you; these things are not coming from God. The prophetic word we receive from the Lord is formed within our spirits.

Prophecy is conditional! It is based on what a person does or does not do. If you do not follow the conditions of a prophetic word, it will not be fulfilled. Jeremiah said he tried not to speak the word he was given, but it was like a fire shut up in his bones, and he could not keep silent (see Jeremiah 20:9). You must respond in obedience. Any disobedience to a word you are given will cancel it. It will not and cannot be fulfilled. Certain conditions must be met first—especially if God has given you instructions on what to do and how to do it. Even if God says that He wants to bless you, if your life is not in order and you are not meeting the conditions, then God cannot bless you. God cannot bless disorder in your life. The Bible says that God chose Saul to be king over Israel, but afterward He turned, saying it pained Him to do it because of Saul's actions and disobedience toward God. Saul changed the conditions. You can reset the proper conditions by choosing total obedience.

One painfully obvious example of this point is the book of Jonah. God called him to speak a word to Nineveh, but he would not have it. He decided to run from God instead. But did that work? Jonah's disobedience caused calamity for himself and others. Yet when he was obedient and he shared the word he was given, the whole city of Nineveh repented and believed in the Lord. There was much fruit for his obedience, and the people of that city were freed from their spiritual bonds.

There is no new revelation, only that which was hidden and is now brought to light. As a prophet, you are not rewriting the Bible, nor are you adding to it or taking from it. You are not John the revelator or Moses writing the Ten Commandments. Everything that needs to be brought to light has already been given. God's Word is the ultimate light: "For with you is the fountain of life; in your light we see light" (Psalm 36:9).

Thus there are limitations to prophecy. You can only go so far in the prophetic, and some things God purposely conceals from us, never letting us see. The famous Christian doxology says, "Oh, the depths of the riches of the wisdom and knowledge of God! How unsearchable his judgments, and his paths beyond tracing out!" (Romans 11:33).

Faith is essential in receiving anything from God. The testing of the prophetic word is a testing of your faith. And the prophet is not the ultimate voice—God is! He supersedes the voice of any prophet. If a prophet has said something to you that you know is not true (is not coming from God), go to God and ask *Him* what He is saying. He is the ultimate Voice.

8

The Difference between
a Prophet and a Psychic

Neutralize the Psychic and Release the Prophetic!

> *Prophecy is the voice of God released to re-create
> and realign.*

We are living in a time when the Lord is pouring out His Spirit upon all flesh! The Word says, "Your sons and daughters will prophesy" (Joel 2:28). Why are they going to prophesy? So that God's voice can reach every tribe and nation. God desires to cover the whole earth with the knowledge of the glory of God even as the waters cover the sea.

Prophets use what I like to call "God's legal avenue," which is through Christ Jesus. He is our Mediator between God and man. As God raises up prophets to declare and decree to individuals, corporations, families and churches, Satan releases his voice to counteract the will and purpose of God in the earth. A prophet is

11

one whom God has anointed to speak on His behalf. A psychic is one whom the devil sends to block the blessing of God in the earth and deliver a word that is contrary to the plans of God for His people.

It is important not to receive a word simply because some individual says he is a prophet and is prophesying into your life. Psychics are very accurate in the things that they say. They can also speak into your life, but they are functioning under demonic influence; therefore, you must discern the source of the word spoken over your life.

God can put a false prophet, such as a psychic, in your midst. Even some people of God consult psychics, notably King Saul. When the prophet Samuel had died and King Saul faced trouble with the Philistines, he asked the Lord for an answer and received none. Then, he decided to consult a psychic (see 1 Samuel 28). Though it was illegal and hypocritical, Saul broke the rules. But beware: Something will always be required of you for illegally obtaining that information. We cannot know what would have been Saul's fate, but we do know that he was given a death sentence. The psychic called up Samuel, who told Saul that he and his sons would be dead the next day.

God speaks through the mouths of His true prophets. God does not speak through the mouths of psychics. Even when Saul consulted the psychic, she did not prophesy from her own wisdom. Her vision was limited to what the true prophet Samuel said through the Spirit of God. Prophecy does not emanate through the soul; it comes from the Spirit. Unless you listen in the spiritual realm, you cannot receive the counsels of the Lord.

Matthew 7:15 says, "Watch out for false prophets. They come to you in sheep's clothing, but inwardly they are ferocious wolves." Satan usually requires your soul in exchange for information. In contrast, when God sends a prophet into your midst, there is not necessarily any form of payment on your part. God will simply speak to your situation. He may require something from you, but not necessarily.

When a prophet speaks, he will always speak a word from the Lord that brings hope, joy and peace, which can only come from the Kingdom of God. Even when it comes as a "hard" word, it is filled with compassion and the Spirit of truth.

Psychics, by contrast, speak on behalf of the enemy. When it is a "positive" word, it is flattery, and when it is negative, it is in the spirit of the accuser of the brethren (Satan; see Revelation 12:10). John 10 records a parable about entering in "by the gate." This speaks of legally walking through the door of heaven and receiving something from the Lord that will be everlasting. The thief takes information that does not belong to him. Prophets come in legally and take what is given freely to God's people in the Spirit. Psychics go into the spirit realm and steal information that they have no right to, and it comes out as either flattery or accusation.

When information is breathed on by the Holy Spirit, it produces revelation! A psychic can only bring information, not revelation. Revelation comes from God alone. Many people do not understand that a prophet speaks of God's perfect will for their lives, while a psychic brings forth only information. Information has no true power, but revelation will enlighten you and open the doors of your life that have been shut so that you may come alive again.

Jesus said that if you enter by any other way besides Him, you are a thief and a robber (see John 10:1). Psychics steal what does not belong to them, while prophets of God drink freely from the mouth of God through Jesus. Prophets are sent with the word of God in their mouths, not as empty shells but full of hope and a message of a bright future.

A psychic's "information" holds the power of death, emptiness and despair, and it is void. As God raises up true prophets, you will also see an increase in the medium and psychic world. But we can rest assured that the true will win out over the counterfeit. God said the knowledge of His glory would cover the earth. He did not say, "I will cover some nations, but others I won't." No! He said, "The earth will be filled with the knowledge of the glory of the LORD"! (Habakkuk 2:14).

If you receive a word from a so-called prophet and you are unsure of the source or the mouthpiece, consider the character of the person who gave it to you. Are they trustworthy? This sounds like a simple enough question, but it can be overlooked! Do you know this person? Have they proven themselves, not only by giving accurate words, but by living a life of the Spirit? What does their character suggest? Are they emotionally mature and psychologically stable people who are growing in Christ?

There are several keys to discerning if a word is right or wrong, legitimate or illegitimate. These questions are straightforward and vital to gaining wisdom:

1. Does this word coincide with the Word of God in Scripture?
2. Does the word glorify or give testimony to the person of Jesus Christ?
3. Is the word consistent with other words or with present realities?
4. Does it come to pass?

First, it is not a true prophecy if the word does not coincide with Scripture. Granted, a word of prophecy may not be a direct quotation from Scripture, and it does not have to be. But does the heart of the message—the main point of the prophecy—agree with scriptural principles and things we know to be true about God?

Second, does it glorify or give testimony to the person of Jesus? Is the word harsh or condemning? Then it is *not* from the Lord. None of His words pronounce condemnation. Judgment, rebuke, correction and encouragement are His main points of communication. But He will never speak to us in a condemning tone, because this is not the person of Jesus. His heart for us is always love.

Third, is the word consistent with reality or other prophecies? If it does not make any logical sense, then it may be an illogical or untrue prophecy.

Fourth, does the word come to pass? This is my favorite principle of prophecy, because it is so clear. As it says in Deuteronomy 18:21–22:

You may say to yourselves, "How can we know when a message has not been spoken by the LORD?" If what a prophet proclaims in the name of the LORD does not take place or come true, that is a message the LORD has not spoken. That prophet has spoken presumptuously, so do not be alarmed.

Lastly, I encourage you to be aware of the testimony of the Spirit to your own heart. When you have gained enough wisdom and experience in the ministry of prophecy, this may be more easily discerned. We see this in the two disciples to whom Jesus appeared on the road following His resurrection. He walked with them, though they did not recognize Him. He explained the Gospel message to them and the fulfillments of prophecies until their eyes were opened and they knew it was the Messiah. When this happened, "He disappeared from their sight. They asked each other, 'Were not our hearts burning within us while he talked with us on the road and opened the Scriptures to us?'" (Luke 24:31–32).

9

Prophesy to Your Situation!

Fill the Atmosphere with Your Prophetic Word!

The prophetic word comes in seed form, packed full of the next chapter of your life.

Then the LORD put forth his hand, and touched my mouth. And the LORD said unto me, Behold, I have put my words in thy mouth.

Jeremiah 1:9, KJV

*Y*ou received the prophetic word. You are pregnant with it, but circumstances around you are causing you to fear. God wants you to prophesy to your circumstances, to whatever is hindering your dream. When we prophesy, it creates an atmosphere of "positive energy." This positive energy is nothing more than the fire of God that has been sent to correct, change or rearrange the situation. When God spoke to Moses to lead the children of Israel

116

out of Egypt, He spoke the "cloud by day" and the "fire by night" into existence. We, as sons of God, speak to the atmosphere of doubt, unbelief and fear and command it to bow in the presence of the voice of the Lord! Remember, the Lord's voice (the word of God) is sharper than any two-edged sword. This "sword" cuts asunder the soul and spirit. This means it brings a separation of the real you (spirit), dividing it from the emotional realm (soul). The soul comprises the mind, will and emotions. When we operate in the soulish realm, it will always bring us to the place of confusion. Always let the voice of the Lord lead, guide and direct you in every situation of life. His voice is the sword of light, direction, guidance, destiny and hope. The Word says, "No weapon formed against you shall prosper" (Isaiah 54:17, NKJV) because the "sword of the Lord" (the prophetic word of the Lord) will shield you from the destruction of the enemy. There truly is power in the "word" (*rhema* or *logos*) of God!

All that God has spoken concerning you is already prepared in the realm of the Spirit. You have to call it in. It only comes in by faith, your title deed of things hoped for. If I give you a title deed, it means that you already have legal ownership. The title deed is the evidence of things not seen.

As Dwayne McLean writes, "You must give expression to the impression. If you say it, it is like a key that opens the door." If God said, "I'm sending you people to help you," begin to call them in from the east, north, south and west. If God said, "Finances are coming," begin to prophesy that the finances shall be here. Name the time that you want the finances to come. As long as God said it, you can name the time when you want the finances to come. Many people just say, "Bless me, Lord." God wants you to name what you desire and then send it in the direction it needs to go to prosper. As long as you are in a covenant with God, you can prophesy and name it. The Greek word for "name" expresses the nature of the thing named. It is time to put a nature to that word God gave you.

The word is in your mouth. The weapons of our warfare are not carnal, but mighty through God to the pulling down of strongholds. Life and death are in the power of the tongue. Begin to prophesy to the strongholds that are preventing your word from coming to pass. When you do, you will see the vision God gave you is going to live and not die. How do you give birth to the word? Begin to sow for it. When you sow financially, give the seed a direction and an assignment. Begin to position your word in the direction it needs to go in order to release your miracle.

You must understand the power of the seed. The prophetic word is your power to unlock your tomorrow. You have more power than your enemies, and you are more powerful than the devil. Jesus said, "I give you the authority . . . over all the power of the enemy" (Luke 10:19, NKJV). You have the power, so nothing shall, by any means, hurt you.

Do not look at your circumstances or at the obstacles. "We look not at the things which are seen, but at the things which are not seen; for the things which are seen are temporal, but the things which are not seen are eternal" (2 Corinthians 4:18, KJV). In other words, our circumstances are subject to change; they are seasonal. The things that are not seen are eternal. Our battle is not with things that are seen, so when God gives us the prophetic word or idea, our response need not be, "God, how can I do that?"

When we see the leaves of the trees begin to move, we are witnessing something unseen—the wind—which is moving the things that are seen. The unseen realm of the Spirit controls the seen realm of our circumstances. One man said, "If the devil left the earth, I'd be sad." Why? Because there would be no one to beat up on. Satan is our punching bag, for we have power over him. He is here to give us practice using our weapons. If you had a son or daughter whom you loved and you sent them against an enemy, would you equip them with less power than the enemy? Of course not!

There is a difference between seeking first the Kingdom of God and seeking God. Many times the Church has God but does not operate in principles of the Kingdom. The world, in fact, operates more in the principles of the Kingdom of God than the Church does. *Kingdom* means "King's domain." It runs by rules and laws, just as our world does. If we follow the rules and laws of God, we will be successful.

A God-given idea will produce wealth, for money chases good ideas. This idea that God has given you, regardless of what it is, has wealth connected to it. Some time ago, a person had an idea to sell "pet" rocks. Now, he is making millions. Whatever ideas God has given to you, you can bring them to pass—just do not share them with small-minded people.

If you want financial prosperity, you must tithe and you must give offerings. Abel brought the firstlings of his flock and the fat thereof. Cain just brought an offering. God had respect for Abel. He respects two things: offerings and faith. On top of that, if you are a leader, your flock must see that you are a tither and a giver. You cannot do it behind the scenes, because they are following your example, and we produce after our kind.

Sow during times of famine. Isaac sowed in famine and received a hundredfold in one year. This helps to bring forth your word, because your word is connected with prosperity. Your prophetic word is connected with your dreams, which are connected with prosperity.

"Beloved, I wish above all things that thou mayest prosper and be in health, even as thy soul prospereth" (3 John 2, KJV). Your soul can only prosper if you are in close fellowship with God. Learn the ways of God. Develop the habit of prayer. If when you arise in the morning you do not feel saved, do not be alarmed. Salvation is not a feeling. You have to know that you know that you know you are saved, and keep walking.

Your assignment was determined before you were born. Jesus said, "You did not choose me, but I chose you" (John 15:16). Many times, the voice of doubt and unbelief is overbearing. The enemy whispers in our ears, "You are not chosen. You are not called. Who told you you were anointed? You can't possibly compare." The same devil said to Jesus, "If thou be the Son of God . . ." Now, if he is going to tempt Jesus, he will do the same thing to you. So when temptation comes, rejoice. Satan is the father of lies—he cannot tell the truth. Whatever he whispers, it is a lie, and you must not believe it.

Know the word and the dream that God has given you. That is why God told Habakkuk to write the prophetic word down. He had to see it before him. What we behold, we become. Write your prophecies down. Every day rehearse them, and they will come to pass.

Time does not mean anything with God. He is the eternal time-keeper. Prove all things; hold fast to that which is good. And get ready to embrace your dream; it is about to come to pass. Before long, you will not be thinking of the time when you heard, "Thus saith the Lord"; you will finally be at the end of your birthing, saying, "And it came to pass." Make your dream, prophecy or vision alive every day by feeding it, seeing it and hearing it out of your own mouth. Speak to yourself so you can hear it. And soon you will have it!

10

Hearing God for Yourself

*God's word comes for you to conceive it
so you can achieve it.*

The greatest experience I could ever have is to hear the voice of my Father, no matter what He says or what He asks of me. This is the source of my happiness.

Having an Ear to Hear God Yourself

There are several different ways we hear God. One is through reading the Scriptures. Another is through the gift of prophecy, operating through mature believers in the Church. Perhaps the most powerful kind of prophecy is the one you receive from God directly, for yourself. When we have revelation about the love of God and our hearts have learned how wonderful and caring He really is toward us, then we can draw near to Him and begin to hear what He might be saying to us. Jesus promised to speak to us personally. "My sheep hear My voice, and I know them, and they follow Me," Jesus said in John 10:27 (NKJV). If you are not hearing His voice, are you really one of His sheep? Or is it that you just have trouble listening?

I believe that everything in this life begins with a thought, including hearing from God. If our thoughts are negative and full of hopelessness, they will become tools of the devil to bring us discouragement and defeat. We feel like quitting, giving up, doing nothing and sometimes backsliding from fellowship with Jesus and returning to a life of sin. We will end up doing the very negative thing that we are "seeing" in our hearts.

If, on the other hand, our thoughts are full of vision and expectant hope, then we engage our feelings, faith and resources, and we begin to take action toward finding a solution to life's problems. God, knowing the importance of the thoughts and intents of the heart, wants to speak vision and truth into each of us to produce faith and fruitfulness.

In 1 Corinthians 13:13 we read, "And now abide faith, hope, love, these three; but the greatest of these is love" (NKJV). Love is primary, but everything we receive from God, we receive by faith. Vision will generate hope, so that faith can take us forward. This is why God wants to put a dream or vision in our hearts. It is an important function of prophecy. If there is no dream and no vision, then hope and faith are not operating, either.

It is important to be calm when trying to listen to the Spirit. He has promised to speak to us. He has told us that His sheep know His voice. As you seek to listen to Him, try to "dial down" emotionally. Ask Him for calm and peace, and that you would not have simply your own feelings but be filled with His thoughts and His heart. Trust Him to speak to you, and rest in His presence. When we hear from the Lord, as His children, there is never a spirit of fear. You will know when He is the one speaking, because He will confirm Himself with His peaceful presence.

If you are uneasy or still unsure about a word or your promptings, talk them out with someone else. Sometimes God gives the interpretation to another person, so that the Body of Christ can be used as a unit.

Hearing God through Someone Else

Prophetic ministry occurred throughout Old Testament Scripture. In Israel the office of the prophet was different than in the New Testament. In the Old Testament, His word became the only voice of God to the nation. As a nation, they required vocal leadership, so God gave them judges to speak for Him. When this was not enough for the people—when they were not satisfied—He gave them kings. Moses, Joshua, Samuel, Elijah, Elisha and others gave direction, pronounced blessing and spoke judgment over the country.

In this day, it is difficult to imagine obeying a leader and trusting him to speak the words of God. Relying on judges and prophets for instruction required much faith and trust. Yet throughout the Old Testament, it would seem to be God's forte to speak through one person for the benefit of thousands.

New Testament prophets revealed Jesus through their words, speaking edification, blessing and insights into coming events with the purpose of encouraging the Body. This began on the Day of Pentecost and continued throughout the New Testament age, and this is our model for the Church today. While we are not all prophets, Scripture teaches that we can all prophesy (see 1 Corinthians 14). In Acts 11:28, Agabus prophesied by the Holy Spirit that there would be a great famine throughout all the world, which happened in the days of Claudius Caesar. In Acts 21:10–11, the same man prophesied the arrest and trial of the apostle Paul. In verse 9 of this same chapter, we read of Philip the evangelist's four daughters, who were prophetesses. Obviously, the early Church had a place for this kind of ministry.

Do Not Quench the Word

Ever wonder why the Scripture admonishes, "Do not quench the Spirit. Do not despise prophecies. Test all things; hold fast what is good" (1 Thessalonians 5:19–21, NKJV)? It is because we sometimes back away from the supernatural expression of the Holy Spirit's communication. Perhaps we have had a bad experience with it and we are now afraid; but as we see prophetic words restore life to a congregation by bringing hope and vision, it will encourage us to not despise but rather love these words that prove so helpful. And when a prophet makes a mistake and is humbly open to correction with a teachable spirit, it also gives us peace and freedom to trust them again for the next time, allowing all of us to learn by his or her mistake.

Prophetic words given in humility, coming from a clean heart, can have tremendous power to build up all of us. This is the kind of word that rests in our hearts, the kind that we can wrap our faith around and believe God for it to happen.

11

Interpreting Prophecy

*God plants His prophetic word in you as a seed so He can
reap His harvest of what you were called and created to do
in the earth.*

ould it be the "gift of interpretation" is the gift of understanding the mysteries and secrets of God? May we possess that
gift to walk in the Christ-conscious mind to understand what is
being said and fashioned in the heavenlies.

The Language of the Prophetic Word

"The heart and soul of the Christian life is learning to hear the voice
of God and developing the courage to do it," said Steve Nicholson,
senior pastor of the Vineyard Christian Church of Evanston.

God brings prophecy into the Church to encourage, exhort
and bless His people. It is one of His ways of speaking something

directly to His people. This can happen through an individual in the church or through a minister whom God brings in.

Just as God can speak to a church through prophecy, He can also use it to speak to an individual. Many Christians, anxious to hear from God, will go seeking someone who can bring them a word of personal prophecy. These same people, who feel they desperately need to hear from God, will often ignore the opportunities to hear from Him through prayer or His Word.

How Personal Prophecy Arrives

Prophecy comes in different ways to different people operating under a prophetic anointing. Although all prophesy to accomplish the same goal, the methodology may vary from individual to individual. Some prophets (or people operating in the gift of prophecy) will hear words within their spirits. Some will see an image or vision that speaks into a situation. Still others will have the words printed out for them, as if printed on a screen. People who seem to be visually oriented or artistic will often see pictures. Others will see or hear words or phrases passing through their mind. I have a friend who is a writer, and she often sees phrases pass through her mind's eye as on a ticker tape or like an airplane advertisement. For others still, they may feel something within their bodies. A physical sensation, pain, tingling or temperature change can all be signals of the Spirit's presence attempting to give you a prophetic word.

No matter how an individual receives the prophecy, it will usually be incomplete. God will not show every detail of a person's life, or even every detail pertaining to the situation. There will only be enough information to express whatever God is wanting to say. We will not have the whole story until we are made complete in Christ, when the Kingdom comes in its fullness. For now, we only have parts of the glory.

> Love never fails. But where there are prophecies, they will cease; where there are tongues, they will be stilled; where there is knowledge,

it will pass away. For we know in part and we prophesy in part, but when completeness comes, what is in part disappears. . . . For now we see only a reflection as in a mirror; then we shall see face to face. Now I know in part; then I shall know fully, even as I am fully known.

1 Corinthians 13:8–10, 12

Often the information given by God will be allegorical in nature. Jesus taught the people through parables, and He has not given up speaking this way. Visions from God are especially likely to be pictures that appear to have no direct bearing on the situation, yet they have a meaning that speaks directly to the person's need.

Interpreting Prophecy

There are usually three parts to a prophecy:

1. Revelation: God gets it out in the open.
2. Interpretation: God's word is always correct out of His mouth.
3. Application: The vessel His word comes through is not perfect and can make mistakes.

God always speaks accurately, but we may not always hear Him accurately. Even if the prophet hears God correctly, the prophecy may not be interpreted correctly. Like a cosmic game of "telephone" gone awry, divine messages can get "lost in translation" from person to person. Different ages, cultures and ways of speaking make any human communication full of nuance and multiplicity even in the most mundane times. When you ask an English speaker for a "napkin" in America, you get a small paper or cloth to wipe your mouth or lay across your lap; when you ask for a napkin in England, you get a diaper!

Likewise, we can hear God's insights more or less accurately but make incorrect applications. This does not mean that the prophecy is wrong, just lost in translation! Be sure to try to speak a prophetic word just as you heard it before lending your interpretation. This way, if your interpretation is inaccurate, the original word can be reexamined later. It is in the area of interpretation that most prophetic error is made. If you receive a prophetic word that does not seem to resonate, look at the original prophecy and see if there could be an alternate interpretation.

Sometimes the interpretation error is on the part of the recipient and not the prophet. God can say, "You will have a daughter, and her name shall be Jubilee." To a pregnant woman, this prophecy must obviously be talking about the baby she is carrying. However, God might be saying this about the next child, or even the one after that. Or it could be an allegorical word about a year of the Lord's favor and release. Prophetic interpretation is a dynamic process that requires love and humility from all parties concerned; be sure to hold your interpretations lightly, in a context of loving submission to God.

For God's people to hear and understand His voice, they must embrace the principles of hearing His words, judging His words spoken through others and interpreting what has been heard. If you take these lessons to heart, you will begin to see the power inherent in the words of God released into your life. Releasing that power will, bit by bit, bring the Kingdom of God. It is to that power—the power of the prophetic word—that we now turn.

12

The Power of the Prophetic Word

The move of God is in your prophetic word to keep you from being stagnant.

Choose your words wisely, for they will bring life to some and death to others. It all depends on what spirit you are speaking from. I choose to spark the light inside of every man that I encounter. To speak only words of hope and life that will cause them to want to live and not die. This is truly the source of life (hope) within the prophetic voice.

Powerful Like a Time Bomb!

I want to discuss something that is asked of me all the time, which is, "How powerful is the prophetic word of God?" The reason I want to discuss this subject is simply because the word of the Lord in a person's life is like a time bomb waiting to explode! We think of a prophetic word as simply a message given to someone inspired by God that tells us what is going to happen in our future. Now, that statement is true, but the prophetic word is also deeper and more powerful than that. The prophetic word is nothing less than the power of life and death; it is the power to call things that are not as though they were. When we use it and understand it, the prophetic word will bring the Kingdom of God to the earth, allowing us to fulfill God's will in our lives. It will enable us to fight and win the battles of faith in the earthly realm.

What is the prophetic word? The word *prophetic* concerns future events. Therefore, the words I use concerning future events in my life are prophetic words. We say that words shape our lives every day; if this statement is true, then I can shape my day by what I speak, because the Bible tells us that life and death are in the power of the tongue. By what I say I will either empower my destiny or destroy it. Faith is the component that brings life to what you are saying and allows you to begin to shape your world to resemble the world God has ordained for you. I want to look at some Scriptures about faith and prophetic words. Remember, prophetic words shape my future destiny in God.

> Now faith is the substance of things hoped for, the evidence of things not seen. For by it the elders obtained a good testimony. By faith we understand that the worlds were framed by the word of God, so that the things which are seen were not made of things which are visible.
>
> Hebrews 11:1–3, NKJV

This informs us that faith is real; it has substance and it manifests itself in the earthly realm, which is created by God who is not seen, producing evidence for all to see. Through the vehicle of faith we understand that worlds are created by the word of God. I'm going to operate by the same method, creating my world by the word of God. The English *word* in Hebrews 11:3 is the Greek *rhema*—that which is or has been uttered by the living voice, the spoken word. This means worlds are created by speaking God's word and believing it will happen just as you spoke it. There is a reason I said *believing* instead of *faith,* because believing is faith in action. If the word spoken is active, then my faith must also be active. Faith in action causes you to move from inactivity to actions, which allow things to be accomplished in the earthly realm.

The Power of Agreement

"And since we have the same spirit of faith, according to what is written, 'I believed and therefore I spoke,' we also believe and therefore speak" (2 Corinthians 4:13, NKJV).

In Amos 3:3 a very important question is asked: "Can two walk together, unless they are agreed?" (NKJV). The passage in 2 Corinthians speaks about the connection between what I believe becoming what I speak and what I have heard spoken becoming what I believe. If this is true, what keeps Christianity true to its core convictions? It is because we all have the same spirit of faith leading us in agreement. I must agree with God that I am going to shape my world the way God shaped this world. Agreement is the key!

"Again I say to you that if two of you agree on earth concerning anything that they ask, it will be done for them by My Father in heaven" (Matthew 18:19, NKJV).

"For there are three that bear witness in heaven: the Father, the Word, and the Holy Spirit; and these three are one" (1 John 5:7, NKJV).

Looking at these two Scriptures, we see that there must be agreement in heaven and in earth. Changing what you speak will require total and absolute agreement with what God has said. Once you begin to speak it, those words become like the words of God. I am not saying we are gods. However, I am saying through Jesus' death and resurrection we have the right of a "power of attorney." The power of attorney is the use of His name when I declare, speak and utter God's word to change and shape my world to resemble His world.

The word of God is the law of God; the law of God is the mind of God. There are laws in operation on earth, established by God, that are fixed. We are all subject to the law of gravity, for example. Man can manipulate the natural world to, in effect, supersede that law—such as by building airplanes that can "supersede" the law of gravity. But the law never stops working; it is always there. When the plane lands or, God forbid, runs out of fuel, the law of gravity shows its effect. The word of God is the same way. It is waiting for someone to use it to supersede the law of man on the earth. Poverty, famine, sickness and disease are all effects of the law of man. Some will argue that Satan has caused these things, but he works through man to try to supersede God's rule in the earth. How do we overcome the law of man? By speaking the laws of God. Remember, the Bible tells us His thoughts are higher than our thoughts. The word of God is higher in truth and in power. The word of God is the law of God; when I speak God's word I supersede the laws in the earth. And I invoke diplomatic immunity, because I am a citizen of heaven and an ambassador in the earth. Simply put, me speaking the word places me in agreement with God, which brings the Kingdom to earth to work on my behalf.

Let me paint a picture of the first chapter of Genesis. It is a picture of how perfection gets destroyed, only to be re-created into a place inhabited by man. In many ways Genesis 1:1 resembles our lives. In the beginning it seems like perfection. Everything is in place, nothing is disturbed.

Genesis 1:2 resembles our lives also. As we grow, we find our lives to be without form and void, just like the earth in this portion of Scripture. Our lives often parallel the Bible; our perfect life is often devastated and affected by people and events outside our control. These things can bring us to a place of emptiness and leave us without direction. But we also see redemption in this passage. Redemption and change were waiting to happen because the Spirit of God was waiting to be called into action.

Many students of the Bible believe that between verse 1 and verse 2 of Genesis 1, Satan was kicked out of heaven and came to the earthly realm, bringing devastation and destruction to the earth that was once perfect. Therefore, in keeping with our theme of the power of the prophetic word, let's begin by analyzing the re-creation process and applying those truths to the process of creating our world through the prophetic word. Genesis 1:3 is a statement of intended thought released by an omnipotent God who verbalizes His intentions as a means of getting things done. God, by declaring, "Let there be light," has set a pattern and method for His children for impacting the earthly realm simply by speaking. Now, to get the impact of Genesis 1:3, the process begins in verse 2: "And the Spirit of God moved upon the face of the waters" (KJV). The word *moved* actually means "to hover or cover," so it should read that the Spirit of God hovered on the face of the waters. As believers we must understand that God knows that re-creating our world is a difficult proposition, so He sent the Comforter, the Holy Spirit, to help us.

It is important to know that the Holy Spirit is in the proper position to help us, but He is waiting on a command; He is waiting on us to say something. The word *Comforter* means "helper." The Holy Spirit helps us, but we must be the administrator; we must give the commands. This is the key point to understand when the Holy Spirit is properly positioned in our lives—all we have to do is take authority! The authority that the Lord has given us allows prophetic people to do prophetic things, to call those things that do not exist into existence by the power of the spoken declarative word.

The Holy Spirit is hovering around you, awaiting instructions to act. In Genesis 1:3, God said, "Let there be light"; the spoken word was carried out by the Holy Spirit exactly as instructed. We do not know the time frame, but we do know the result; the result was light, which we understand and believe by faith. In my life, when I speak, I do not know the time frame, but by faith I know the expected results of the prophetic words that I used to shape and change my world.

13

Stand on the Word God Gave You!

Are you listening? He is speaking.

When life is hard and the road is long, be assured a voice will always speak within, saying, "My yoke is easy, and My burden is light." This is the voice that brings strength to the body, that says, "You can do it and I will see to it."

Pick Up Your Sword and Fight!

After God had established Jehoshaphat as king of Judah, he faced a crisis: the coming onslaught of the armies of the Moabites and Ammonites. Jehoshaphat's response was to seek the Lord to know what to do. In the events that followed, we see the powerful effects of the response that God gave.

> [Jehoshaphat] went to GOD for help and ordered a nationwide fast. The country of Judah united in seeking GOD's help—they came from all the cities of Judah to pray to GOD.

Then Jehoshaphat took a position before the assembled people of Judah and Jerusalem at The Temple of GOD in front of the new courtyard and said, "O GOD, God of our ancestors, are you not God in heaven above and ruler of all kingdoms below? You hold all power and might in your fist—no one stands a chance against you! . . . And now they've come to kick us out of the country you gave us. O dear God, won't you take care of them? We're helpless before this vandal horde ready to attack us. We don't know what to do; we're looking to you."

Everyone in Judah was there—little children, wives, sons—all present and attentive to GOD.

Then Jahaziel was moved by the Spirit of GOD to speak from the midst of the congregation. (Jahaziel was the son of Zechariah, the son of Benaiah, the son of Jeiel, the son of Mattaniah the Levite of the Asaph clan.) He said . . . "GOD's word: Don't be afraid; don't pay any mind to this vandal horde. This is God's war, not yours. . . . You won't have to lift a hand in this battle; just stand firm, Judah and Jerusalem, and watch GOD's saving work for you take shape. Don't be afraid, don't waver. March out boldly tomorrow—GOD is with you."

Then Jehoshaphat knelt down, bowing with his face to the ground. All Judah and Jerusalem did the same, worshiping GOD. The Levites (both Kohathites and Korahites) stood to their feet to praise GOD, the God of Israel; they praised at the top of their lungs!

They were up early in the morning, ready to march into the wilderness of Tekoa. As they were leaving, Jehoshaphat stood up and said, "Listen Judah and Jerusalem! Listen to what I have to say! Believe firmly in GOD, your God, and your lives will be firm! Believe in your prophets and you'll come out on top!"

After talking it over with the people, Jehoshaphat appointed a choir for GOD; dressed in holy robes, they were to march ahead of the troops, singing,

Give thanks to GOD, His love never quits.

As soon as they started shouting and praising, GOD set ambushes against the men of Ammon, Moab, and Mount Seir as they were attacking Judah, and they all ended up dead. The Ammonites and Moabites mistakenly attacked those from Mount Seir and massacred them. Then, further confused, they went at each other, and all ended up killed.

As Judah came up over the rise, looking into the wilderness for the horde of barbarians, they looked on a killing field of dead bodies—not a living soul among them.

When Jehoshaphat and his people came to carry off the plunder they found more loot than they could carry off—equipment, clothing, valuables. It took three days to cart it away! On the fourth day they came together at the Valley of Blessing (Beracah) and blessed GOD (that's how it got the name, Valley of Blessing).

Jehoshaphat then led all the men of Judah and Jerusalem back to Jerusalem—an exuberant parade. GOD had given them joyful relief from their enemies! They entered Jerusalem and came to The Temple of GOD with all the instruments of the band playing.

When the surrounding kingdoms got word that GOD had fought Israel's enemies, the fear of God descended on them. Jehoshaphat heard no more from them; as long as Jehoshaphat reigned, peace reigned.

> 2 Chronicles 20:3–6, 11–15, 17–30,
> THE MESSAGE, emphasis mine

In this passage we see that King Jehoshaphat knew how to war according to the word of the Lord spoken by Jahaziel. When the Lord began to speak to him, he knew he was to obey that word completely. He began to stir up his faith to do whatever the Lord asked of him. He knew the blessings of God would overshadow him and that all of his enemies would be defeated because he obeyed the word of the Lord that was given to him.

To the natural mind, Jehoshaphat's instructions to the people sound a bit crazy. Anybody will tell you that sounds, music and singing will not stop guns, swords or any weapon headed toward you. But 1 Corinthians 1:27 says, "But God hath chosen the foolish things of the world to confound the wise; and God hath chosen the weak things of the world to confound the things which are mighty" (KJV).

I want you to consider carefully something about the Israelites. They were prepared by the finest "schools" in warfare and battle strategies and techniques. They knew how to "fight the good fight of faith" and win! They had been taught and trained and were ready to fight at any given time. Yet God had other plans for them when it came to this certain battle. God had a strategic plan for them to "listen to the voice of the good Shepherd" and heed it. He wanted to show them the power of His voice when He speaks. He wanted them to understand that His word works and that it does not return to Him void; it accomplishes all that He sends it to do. His plan was for them to release their faith in the *rhema* word of the Lord—put another way, His spoken, spontaneous voice.

We must inquire of the Lord in every area of our lives. We are led by His voice. The Bible says that we know the voice of the Shepherd, and the voice of a stranger we will not follow (see John 10:4–5). Just because yesterday's strategies for battle worked then does not mean that they will work today or tomorrow. He knows what is needed in every situation of our lives. Too many times we rely on past battle plans instead of paying the price in prayer to receive a fresh plan for today.

If you could only have seen all of these warriors on the battlefield, weapons in hand and ready for war! They already knew the "hows" and the "whys" of this battle. They eagerly awaited the approach of the enemy. The closer the enemy came, the sooner the payoff of their natural training.

I imagine this great, vast army was somewhat like we see in the movies: huge men with armor and swords ready to destroy anything that moved. As the enemy advanced, they were in place. All of a sudden, the Lord brought a "shift" into the atmosphere, and everything they knew began to change. That sounds just like God, does it not? He always messes up our plans to bring us a better one. We might not know it is a better plan at first, but He always desires for us to trust Him completely with our lives. When the strategy of heaven enters the room, everything as we once knew it will change. God is good about bringing a change to your atmosphere.

The Lord told the army not to fight but stand. It reminds me of Ephesians 6:13: "Therefore put on the full armor of God, so that when the day of evil comes, you may be able to stand your ground, and after you have done everything, to stand." So they were told to stand still while the "choir" sang. *What? That makes no sense, God! This is not correct protocol for battle. We fight first!*

But God said, "I know the ending from the beginning, and I know what needs to take place first." Why? So He can show us how much we need to listen and pay attention to His voice.

Something I love about this story is Jahaziel himself. The text tells us he was a descendant of Asaph, the prophet and psalmist known for penning Psalm 50 and Psalms 73–83. As a descendant of a prophet, Jahaziel accepted the mantle of the prophet. Asaph is known for being a singing prophet, one who prophesied accompanied by harps, flutes and lyres (see 1 Chronicles 25:1–2; Psalm 81:1–2). After Jahaziel's prophecy of the Lord's strength and deliverance, the people of Judah and Jerusalem paraded back to the Temple with songs and instruments, just as in the days of old. Jahaziel was operating in the legacy of his prophetic gifting.

Many people fail at spiritual warfare for one important reason: instead of trusting in the Lord and obeying His word, they begin to lean on their own understanding, failing to acknowledge Him in all their ways. Just about the time the Lord is ready to come through and perform a miracle on their behalf, they decide to draw their swords and wage war in the flesh. But not Jehoshaphat! He and his people stood still, as the Lord had told them to do. They trusted in the Lord and obeyed His prophetic word that was given to them, and victory began to happen!

What was the secret to their success? Trusting the Lord and obeying His word, no matter what.

Now Elisha had been suffering from the illness from which he died. Jehoash king of Israel went down to see him and wept over him. "My father! My father!" he cried. "The chariots and horsemen of Israel!"

Elisha said, "Get a bow and some arrows," and he did so. "Take the bow in your hands," he said to the king of Israel. When he had taken it, Elisha put his hands on the king's hands.

"Open the east window," he said, and he opened it. "Shoot!" Elisha said, and he shot. "The LORD's arrow of victory, the arrow of

victory over Aram!" Elisha declared. "You will completely destroy
the Arameans at Aphek."

2 Kings 13:14–17

You will notice that the prophetic word was delivered to the king
of Israel. He was given an opportunity to make the shift, to war
according to the prophetic word God had given him.

> Then he said, "Take the arrows," and the king took them. Elisha
> told him, "Strike the ground." He struck it three times and stopped.
> The man of God was angry with him and said, "You should have
> struck the ground five or six times; then you would have defeated
> Aram and completely destroyed it. But now you will defeat it only
> three times."

2 Kings 13:18–19

The king began to wage war according to the instruction of the
Lord. If you notice, the king had to keep on "pressing toward the
mark," signaled in the spiritual and manifesting in physical victory.

Whenever we step out to fight for those things the Lord has
spoken to us about, we must never give up, no matter how long
it takes! We must keep on fighting, keep on praying and keep on
reaching toward the prize of the high call in Christ Jesus. Remember, if there is a "high call," then there must be a "low call." Which
road are you traveling? Are you pressing through, or are you just
settling for anything that comes your way in life? God has given
us a plan for our lives to better our lives from poverty to riches,
from death unto life and from glory to glory. Jesus said, "I came
that they may have life, and have it abundantly" (John 10:10, NASB).
God will speak His word to you through prophecy about the *zoe*
kind of life (the God kind of life) He wants you to have, but the
rest of it is up to you. You have to "make it happen." You have to
call those things that are not as though they were.

This is why we have a sword, a shield and the other weapons of
warfare to "make it happen." You cannot war for just three days
and then give up. Keep warring until every enemy has become

your footstool! Do not let doubt, unbelief or fear stand in your way. Fight until the breakthrough comes. God is the "Lord of the breakthrough." Stand firm, stand strong, stand bold and watch the salvation of the Lord come to you. The prophetic word is sharp and powerful, sharper than any two-edged sword. Use it wisely with faith and you will overcome every time. The sword of the Lord is the word of God! Take up your "prophetic sword" (word) and sling it toward the enemy who told you that you would never win, you would never overcome and you could never have the finer things in life. This is your moment to make the shift happen. If God has promised you something through a prophetic word, do not stop; start living by confessing what God said to you, decreeing that it will come to pass. And finally, walk it out by "dressing the part"; treat the prophetic word as if it has already happened!

Many times in my own life, I have had to literally dress the part, talk the part and act like I already have become what God said I am. There is an old saying, "Fake it till you make it." This is so true. Fake it, if you have to, until it manifests in the natural realm and you truly become it.

Intimacy and Action

At the end of the day, life in the prophetic is a life of *intimacy* and *action*. In Old Covenant times, prophets were the servants of God; this was a high honor. But under the New Covenant, our honor is even greater! Jesus says, "I no longer call you servants, because a servant does not know his master's business. Instead, I have called you friends, for everything that I learned from my Father I have made known to you" (John 15:15).

Friendship. Getting to know Jesus daily, abiding in the outflowing life of the Trinity (which is the context of Jesus' statement above—take a moment to read John 15 in its entirety), bears the same fruit that hanging out with *anyone* yields—you become friends! You tell friends things that you do not tell total strangers or even casual acquaintances; friends know your hopes, dreams and secrets. It is no different with the counsel of God. Thanks to His freely offered gift of grace, we can now approach God's throne room boldly (see Hebrews 4:16), talking to Him—and hearing from Him. I have written a companion book, *The Power of the Eternal Now,* which goes deeper into illuminating our firsthand, present-tense walk with God from which friendship springs.

Have you ever had a friend who did not really *listen* to you—and who never did what you wanted to do? They were probably not your friend for long! You still love and care for them, but if they consistently miss appointments for your get-togethers, if they dominate your conversations by talking about themselves all the time and glaze over when you are sharing *your* heart, and if they never take action when you invite them to things you are both (supposedly) passionate about, they cannot rightly remain in the "friend" category for long. The same is true with Jesus.

In John 15, Jesus continues, "You did not choose me, but I chose you and appointed you so that you might go and bear fruit—fruit that will last—and so that whatever you ask in my name the Father will give you. This is my command: Love each other" (John 15:16–17). Authentic friendship bears the fruit of friendship—joint endeavors emerge and a track record of the friendship is established, a kind of public testimony of your collaboration—your *co-labor-ation*, as the apostle Paul might have said. Would it not be cool if you and Jesus—or your church and Jesus—became known as a hyphenated name in your city, kind of like we do with celebrity romances (*Bennifer* or *Brangelina*)? What if you abided in God so closely and took action on what the Spirit shared in His throne room so consistently that you became known as *JesusElizabeth,* or *Christ-opher*?

Let's be doers of the word, as James encouraged us (see James 1:22), not mere prophetic hobbyists, hearing divine mysteries and saying, "Isn't that nice!" Christ is the vine and we are the branches; God has called us to be manifestations—leaves—of the Tree of Life, for the healing of the nations (see Revelation 22:2). Our prophetic vocation makes us a people of divine intimacy and action—not for our personal amusement or even for our personal growth, but to join God in His new creation work of healing the world. It is a high priestly vocation, the times are urgent and our loving Creator has equipped us for every good work (see 2 Timothy 3:17).

Are you ready? Let's listen together!

About Jeremy Lopez

Dr. Jeremy Lopez is founder and president of Identity Network International (www.identitynetwork.net), an apostolic and prophetic resource website that reaches well over 150,000 people around the globe, distributing books and audio teachings on the prophetic move of God. Jeremy has prophesied to thousands of people from all walks of life, including producers, investors, business owners, attorneys, city leaders, musicians, congregations and various ministries around the world, concerning areas such as finding missing children, financial breakthroughs, parenthood and life-changing decisions.

Dr. Jeremy is an international teacher and motivational speaker, speaking on new dimensions of revelatory knowledge in Scripture, universal laws, mysteries, patterns and cycles. His life and ministry are marked by a love for all people and desire to enrich their lives with love, grace and the mercy of God. He believes this is the hour for the sons of God to arise. This ministry is for seeing every believer awake to his or her destiny. Dr. Jeremy believes it is time to awaken to the fullness of our God-given divine consciousness and live a life filled with potential, purpose and destiny.

Dr. Jeremy teaches the principle that we are positioned in heavenly places and are called to minister out of that realm. He shares this vision in conferences, prophetic meetings and church services. He serves on many governing boards, speaks to business leaders across the nation and holds a doctor of divinity degree from Saint Thomas Christian College in Florida. He has ministered in many nations, including Jamaica, Indonesia, Haiti, Hong Kong, Taiwan, the United Kingdom, Mexico, Singapore, Costa Rica and the Bahamas. He has hosted and been a guest on radio programs in locations from Indonesia to New York.

He is the author of *The Power of the Eternal Now* and *The Law of Financial Progression,* and he has recorded over forty audio teachings. Jeremy's ministry has been recognized by many other prophetic leaders around the nation.

You can visit Jeremy's website for more resources and sign up for his e-mail newsletters and prophetic words at www.identitynetwork.net. You may contact us by e-mail at Customerservice@identitynetwork.net.